AAT

DEVOLVED ASSESSMENT KIT

Intermediate Unit 7

Reports and Returns

August 2000 edition

- Practice activities

- Two practice devolved assessments

- Two trial run devolved assessments

- The AAT's sample simulation for this Unit

- Index of practice activities

FOR 2000 AND 2001 DEVOLVED ASSESSMENTS

BPP Publishing
August 2000

First edition May 1998
Third edition August 2000

ISBN 0 7517 6239 3 (Previous edition 0 7517 6157 5)

British Library Cataloguing-in-Publication Data
A catalogue record for this book
is available from the British Library

Published by

BPP Publishing Limited
Aldine House, Aldine Place
London W12 8AW

www.bpp.com

Printed in Great Britain by W M Print
Frederick Street
Walsall
West Midlands WS2 9NE

We are grateful to the Lead Body for Accounting for permission to reproduce extracts from the Standards of Competence for Accounting.

INTRODUCTION (v)

How to use this Devolved Assessment Kit – Unit 7 Standards of Competence - Assessment strategy

BPP PUBLISHING

HOW TO USE THIS DEVOLVED ASSESSMENT KIT

Aims of this Devolved Assessment Kit

> To provide the knowledge and practice to help you succeed in the devolved assessment for Intermediate Unit 7 *Preparing Reports and Returns*

To pass the devolved assessment you need a thorough understanding in all areas covered by the standards of competence.

> To tie in with the other components of the BPP Effective Study Package to ensure you have the best possible chance of success.

Interactive Text

This covers all you need to know for devolved assessment for Unit 7 *Preparing Reports and Returns*. Icons clearly mark key areas of the text. Numerous activities throughout the text help you practise what you have just learnt.

Devolved Assessment Kit

When you have understood and practised the material in the Interactive Text, you will have the knowledge and experience to tackle this Devolved Assessment Kit for Unit 7 *Preparing Reports and Returns*. This aims to get you through the devolved assessment, whether in the form of a simulation or workplace assessment. It contains the AAT's Sample Simulation for Unit 7 plus other simulations.

Recommended approach to this Devolved Assessment Kit

(a) To achieve competence in all units you need to be able to do **everything** specified by the standards. Study the Interactive Text very carefully and do not skip any of it.

(b) Learning is an **active** process. Do **all** the activities as you work through the Interactive Text so you can be sure you really understand what you have read.

(c) After you have covered the material in the Interactive Text, work through this **Devolved Assessment Kit**.

(d) Try the **Practice Activities**. These are short activities, to reinforce your learning and consolidate the practice that you have had doing the activities in the Interactive Text.

(e) Then attempt the **Practice Devolved Assessments**. They are designed to test your competence in certain key areas of the Standards of Competence, but are not as comprehensive as the ones set by the AAT. They are a 'warm-up' exercise, to develop your studies towards the level of full devolved assessment.

(f) Next do the **Trial Run Devolved Assessments**. Although these are not yet fully at the level you can expect when you do a full devolved assessment, they do cover all the performance criteria of the elements indicated.

(g) Finally try the AAT's **Sample Simulation,** which gives you the clearest idea of what a full assessment will be like.

BPP PUBLISHING

Remember this is a **practical** course.

- Try to relate the material to your experience in the workplace or any other work experience you may have had.

- Try to make as many links as you can to your study of the other Units at this level.

UNIT 7 STANDARDS OF COMPETENCE

The structure of the Standards for Unit 7

The Unit commences with a statement of the knowledge and understanding which underpin competence in the unit's elements.

The unit is then divided into elements of competence describing activities which the individual should be able to perform.

Each element includes:

(a) A set of **performance criteria** which define what constitutes competent performance

(b) A **range statement** which defines the situations, contexts, methods etc in which competence should be displayed

(c) **Evidence requirements**, which state that competence must be demonstrated consistently, over an appropriate time scale with evidence of performance being provided from the appropriate sources

(d) **Sources of evidence**, being suggestions of ways in which you can find evidence to demonstrate that competence

The elements of competence for Unit 7 *Preparing Reports and Returns* are set out below. Knowledge and understanding required for the unit as a whole are listed first, followed by the performance criteria, range statements, evidence requirements and sources of evidence for each element. Performance criteria are cross-referenced to chapters in the Unit 7 *Reports and Returns* Interactive Text.

Unit 7 Preparing reports and returns

What is the unit about?

This unit relates to the preparation of reports and returns from information obtained from all relevant sources. You are required to calculate ratios and performance indicators and present the information according to the appropriate conventions and definitions to either management or outside agencies, including the VAT office. The unit is also concerned with your communication responsibilities which include obtaining authorisation before despatching reports, seeking guidance from the VAT office and presenting reports and returns in the appropriate manner.

Knowledge and understanding

The business environment

- Main sources of relevant government statistics (Elements 7.1 & 7.2)

- Awareness of relevant performance and quality measures (Element 7.1)

- Main types of outside organisations requiring reports and returns: regulatory; grant awarding; information collecting; trade associations (Element 7.2)

- Basic law and practice relating to all issues covered in the range statement and referred to in the performance criteria. Specific issues include: the classification of types of supply; registration requirements; the form of VAT invoices; tax points (Element 7.3)

- Sources of information on VAT: Customs and Excise Guide (Element 7.3)

- Administration of VAT: enforcement (Element 7.3)

- Special schemes: annual accounting; cash accounting; bad debt relief (Element 7.3)

Accounting techniques

- Use of standard units of inputs and outputs (Element 7.1 & 7.3)

- Time series analysis (Element 7.1)

- Use of index numbers (Element 7.1)

- Main types of performance indicators: productivity; cost per unit; resource utilisation; profitability (Elements 7.1 & 7.2)

- Ratios: gross profit margin; net profit margin; return on capital employed (Elements 7.1 & 7.2)

- Tabulation of accounting and other quantitative information (Elements 7.1 & 7.2)

- Methods of presenting information: written reports; diagrammatic; tabular (Elements 7.1 & 7.2)

The organisation

- Understanding of the ways the accounting systems of an organisation are affected by its organisational structure, its administrative systems and procedures and the nature of its business transactions (Elements 7.1, 7.2 & 7.3)

- Understanding of the purpose and structure of reporting systems within the organisation (Element 7.1)

- Background understanding that a variety of outside agencies may require reports and returns from organisations and that these requirements must be built into administrative and accounting systems and procedures (Element 7.2 & 7.3)

- Background understanding that recording and accounting practices may vary between organisations and different parts of organisations (Elements 7.1, 7.2 & 7.3)

- An understanding of the basis of the relationship between the organisation and the VAT office (Element 7.3)

Element 7.1   Prepare and present periodic performance reports

Performance criteria	Chapters in the Interactive Text
1 Information derived from different units of the organisation is consolidated into the appropriate form	9
2 Information derived from different information systems within the organisation is correctly reconciled	9
3 When comparing results over time an appropriate method, which allows for changing price levels, is used	7
4 Transactions between separate units of the organisation are accounted for in accordance with the organisation's procedures	10
5 Ratios and performance indicators are accurately calculated in accordance with the organisation's procedures	9, 11
6 Reports are prepared in the appropriate form and presented to management within required timescales	2 – 6, 8

Range statement

1   Information: costs; revenue

2   Ratios: gross profit margin; net profit margin; return on capital employed

3   Performance indicators: productivity; cost per unit; resource utilisation; profitability

4   Methods of presenting information: written report containing diagrams; table

Evidence requirements

- Competence must be demonstrated consistently, over an appropriate timescale with evidence of performance being provided of periodic performance reports.

Sources of evidence

(these are examples of sources of evidence, but you may be able to identify other, appropriate sources)

- **Observed performance**, eg Consolidating information in the appropriate form; reconciling information from different information systems; comparing results over time; calculating ratios and performance indicators; preparing reports; oral presentation of periodic performance reports.

- **Work produced by the candidate**, eg periodic performance reports containing written information, charts and graphs; calculations of ratios and performance indicators; correspondence between different units of the organisation.

- **Authenticated testimonies from relevant witnesses.**

- **Personal accounts of competence, eg report of performance.**

- **Other sources of evidence to prove competence or knowledge and understanding where it is not apparent from performance**, eg performance in independent assessment; performance in simulation; responses to verbal questioning.

Element 7.2   Prepare reports and returns for outside agencies

Performance criteria	Chapters in the Interactive Text
1 Relevant information is identified, collated and presented in accordance with the conventions and definitions used by outside agencies	2, 8
2 Calculations of ratios and performance indicators are accurate	9
3 Authorisation for the despatch of completed reports and returns is sought from the appropriate person	1
4 Reports and returns are presented in accordance with outside agencies' requirements and deadlines	2, 8

Range statement

1   Ratios: gross profit margin; net profit margin; return on capital employed

2   Reports and returns: written report; return on standard form

Evidence requirements

- Competence must be demonstrated consistently, over an appropriate timescale with evidence of performance being provided of reports and returns being presented to outside agencies.

Sources of evidence

(these are examples of sources of evidence, but you may be able to identify other, appropriate sources)

- **Observed performance**, eg collating information; presenting information; preparing information; preparing reports and returns; calculating ratios and performance indicators; seeking authorisation for the despatch of reports and returns.

- **Work produced by the candidate**, eg written reports; standard returns; authorisation for despatch; calculations of ratios and performance indicators; correspondence with outside agencies.

- **Authenticated testimonies from relevant witnesses.**

- **Personal accounts of competence**, eg report of performance.

- **Other sources of evidence to prove competence or knowledge and understanding where it is not apparent from performance**, eg reports and working papers; performance in independent assessment; performance in simulation; responses to questions.

Element 7.3   Prepare VAT returns

Performance criteria	Chapters in the Interactive Text
1 VAT returns are correctly completed using data from the appropriate recording systems and are submitted within the statutory time limits	12
2 Relevant inputs and outputs are correctly identified and calculated	12, 13
3 Submissions are made in accordance with current legislation	13
4 Guidance is sought from the VAT office when required, in a professional manner	13

Range statement

1   Recording systems: computerised ledgers; manual control account; cash book

2   Inputs and outputs: standard supplies; exempt supplies; zero rated supplies; imports; exports

Evidence requirements

- Competence must be demonstrated consistently, with evidence of performance being provided of VAT returns with backup documentary evidence.

Sources of evidence

(these are examples of sources of evidence, but you may be able to identify other, appropriate sources)

- **Observed performance**, eg completing VAT returns; calculating inputs and outputs; seeking guidance from the VAT office.

- **Work produced by the candidate**, eg completed VAT returns; calculating inputs and outputs; seeking guidance from the VAT office.

- **Authenticated testimonies from relevant witnesses.**

- **Personal accounts of competence**, eg report of performance.

- **Other sources of evidence to prove competence or knowledge and understanding where it is not apparent from performance**, eg performance in simulation; performance in independent assessment; responses to questions.

BPP PUBLISHING

ASSESSMENT STRATEGY

This Unit is assessed entirely by means of **devolved assessment**.

Devolved assessment

Devolved assessment is a means of collecting evidence of your ability to **carry out practical activities** and to **operate effectively in the conditions of the workplace** to the standards required. Evidence may be collected at your place of work, or at an Approved Assessment Centre by means of simulations of workplace activity, or by a combination of these methods.

If the Approved Assessment Centre is a **workplace**, you may be observed carrying out accounting activities as part of your normal work routine. You should collect documentary evidence of the work you have done, or contributed to, in an **accounting portfolio**. Evidence collected in a portfolio can be assessed in addition to observed performance or where it is not possible to assess by observation.

Where the Approved Assessment Centre is a **college or training organisation**, devolved assessment will be by means of a combination of the following.

- Documentary evidence of activities carried out at the workplace, collected by you in an **accounting portfolio**.

- Realistic **simulations** of workplace activities. These simulations may take the form of case studies and in-tray exercises and involve the use of primary documents and reference sources.

- **Projects and assignments** designed to assess the Standards of Competence.

If you are unable to provide workplace evidence you will be able to complete the assessment requirements by the alternative methods listed above.

Possible assessment methods

Where possible, evidence should be collected in the workplace, but this may not be a practical prospect for you. Equally, where workplace evidence can be gathered it may not cover all elements. The AAT regards performance evidence from simulations, case studies, projects and assignments as an acceptable substitute for performance at work, provided that they are based on the Standards and, as far as possible, on workplace practice.

There are a number of methods of assessing accounting competence. The list below is not exhaustive, nor is it prescriptive. Some methods have limited applicability, but others are capable of being expanded to provide challenging tests of competence.

Assessment method	Suitable for assessing
Performance of an accounting task either in the workplace or by simulation: eg preparing and processing documents, posting entries, making adjustments, balancing, calculating, analysing information etc by manual or computerised processes	**Basic task competence.** Adding supplementary oral questioning may help to draw out underpinning knowledge and understanding and highlight your ability to deal with contingencies and unexpected occurrences
General case studies. These are broader than simulations. They include more background information about the system and business environment	Ability to **analyse a system** and suggest ways of modifying it. It could take the form of a written report, with or without the addition of oral or written questions
Accounting problems/cases: eg a list of balances that require adjustments and the preparation of final accounts	Understanding of the **general principles of accounting** as applied to a particular case or topic
Preparation of flowcharts/diagrams. To illustrate an actual (or simulated) accounting procedure	**Understanding of the logic** behind a procedure, of controls, and of relationships between departments and procedures. Questions on the flow chart or diagram can provide evidence of underpinning knowledge and understanding
Interpretation of accounting information from an actual or simulated situation. The assessment could include non-financial information and written or oral questioning	**Interpretative competence**
Preparation of written reports on an actual or simulated situation	**Written communication skills**
Analysis of critical incidents, problems encountered, achievements	Your ability to handle **contingencies**
Listing of likely errors eg preparing a list of the main types of errors likely to occur in an actual or simulated procedure	Appreciation of the range of **contingencies** likely to be encountered. Oral or written questioning would be a useful supplement to the list
Outlining the organisation's policies, guidelines and regulations	Performance criteria relating to these aspects of competence. It also provides evidence of competence in **researching information**
Objective tests and short-answer questions	**Specific knowledge**
In-tray exercises	Your **task-management ability** as well as technical competence
Supervisors' reports	**General job competence,** personal effectiveness, reliability, accuracy, and time management. Reports need to be related specifically to the Standards of Competence
Analysis of work logbooks/diaries	**Personal effectiveness,** time management etc. It may usefully be supplemented with oral questioning

Assessment method	Suitable for assessing
Formal written answers to questions	Knowledge and understanding of the **general accounting environment** and its impact on particular units of competence
Oral questioning	**Knowledge and understanding** across the range of competence including organisational procedures, methods of dealing with unusual cases, contingencies and so on. It is often used in conjunction with other methods

Simulations

Simulations will generally be based round a single scenario containing information relevant to all three elements of the Unit. You will need to select the items of information relevant to each task. **Simulations for the new Unit 7 will be approximately 3¹/₂ hours long.**

Practice activities

The following data is required for Practice activities 1-3.

Comma Limited   Income Statement

	September 20X2		Year to date	
	Budget £	Actual £	Budget £	Actual £
Gross sales	2,207,000	2,079,480	23,519,000	24,498,743
Discounts	(64,000)	(60,510)	(684,000)	(703,871)
Net sales	2,143,000	2,018,970	22,835,000	23,794,872
Standard cost	1,123,500	1,022,777	11,567,000	12,314,815
Variances	171,000	241,240	1,888,000	2,271,729
Other costs	187,400	227,004	2,734,000	1,911,008
Inter-company contribution	(119,400)	(178,273)	(1,600,400)	(1,296,234)
Total cost of sales	1,362,500	1,312,748	14,588,600	15,201,318
Manufacturing margin	780,500	706,222	8,246,400	8,593,554
Direct sales	70,000	57,271	682,000	672,827
Promotion	61,000	45,843	632,000	637,221
Other marketing	76,600	73,490	1,172,000	1,247,160
General admin	181,000	181,221	1,997,400	1,886,662
Data processing	68,000	70,147	721,000	713,072
Loan interest	62,000	65,014	710,000	702,942
	518,600	492,986	5,914,400	5,859,884
Inter-company contribution	(40,000)	(20,102)	(490,000)	(189,722)
Total overheads	478,600	472,884	5,424,400	5,670,162
Operating income	301,900	233,338	2,822,000	2,923,392
Inter-company (net)	(19,000)	21,270	(210,000)	(22,972)
Income before taxes	282,900	254,608	2,612,000	2,900,420
Taxes on income	(151,000)	(103,700)	(1,397,000)	(1,411,670)
Net income	131,900	150,908	1,215,000	1,488,750

NET SALES BY GEOGRAPHICAL MARKET

	20X1	20W6
United Kingdom	12,248,721	9,272,845
Canada	1,722,400	1,888,245
Eire	2,014,522	-
Germany	3,604,745	1,457,208
France	2,308,722	1,200,405
Nigeria	1,521,223	1,721,542
Other EC	2,418,717	894,281
USA	3,401,972	2,841,470
Other non-EC	1,182,718	1,141,722
	30,423,740	20,417,718

Note. Eire, Germany and France were all members of the European Union in both 20W6 and 20X1, as was the United Kingdom.

TOTAL NET SALES

	£
20W6	20,417,718
20W7	22,084,165
20W8	23,782,722
20W9	25,621,481
20X0	28,088,390
20X1	30,423,740
20X2 Sept YTD	23,794,872

Average number of employees

	Full-time	Part-time
20W6	694	38
20W7	721	37
20W8	742	44
20W9	765	48
20X0	870	53
20X1	852	57
20X2 Sept YTD	842	61

Practice activity 1

Prepare a simplified income statement for Comma Ltd showing the budgeted and actual results for the month of September 20X2, and the nine months to September 20X2, with both £million (rounded as considered appropriate but with no amount shown to more than three digits) and percentage columns (net sales = 100%; round to the nearest one per cent). The income statement should include the following lines.

> Net sales
> Less: Standard cost
>   Variances
>   Other costs
>   Inter-company contribution
> Manufacturing margin
> Selling expenses
> Administrative expenses
> Inter-company contribution
> Operating income
> Inter-company (net)
> Income before tax
> Tax
> Net income

For the purposes of comparison, your statement should also incorporate the following previous year actual figures, rounded as appropriate and additionally showing the manufacturing margin and operating income expressed as a percentage of net sales.

September 20X1

	£
Net sales	1,850,972
Manufacturing margin	611,227
Operating income	209,944

9 months to September 20X2

	£
Net sales	22,402,106
Manufacturing margin	7,827,435
Operating income	2,210,810

Practice activity 2

Prepare a pie chart comparing the split of Comma Ltd's net sales between its major geographical markets in 20W6 and 20X1. The major geographical markets should be classified as follows.

UK
Exports: European Union
               North America
               Other

Practice activity 3

Prepare a bar chart for Comma Ltd showing net sales per full-time employee (in 20X2 pounds) over the period 20W6 to 20X1. A part-time employee is to be treated as equivalent to one half of a full time employee for this purpose. The average Retail Prices Index figures below are to be used for the purpose of adjusting the relevant figures to 20X2 pounds.

Year	RPI average
20W6	128.2
20W7	132.7
20W8	139.5
20W9	146.2
20X0	150.7
20X1	157.8
20X2	164.9

The following data relate to Practice activities 4-10.

EMERALD TAXIS LTD
MANAGEMENT ACCOUNTS
CUMULATIVE REPORT FOR THE SIX MONTHS ENDED 30 JUNE 20X7

Vehicle	1	2	3	4	5	6	7	8	Total
Registration number	J761 SET	K937 SET	H976 WSF	J172 PED	H127 PDM	G789 JDM	J129 HBD	H969 MDD	-
Local authority reference	SC84	SC101	SC105	SC126	SC191	SC213	SC220	SC225	-
Operating mileage	16,100	17,900	15,200	17,500	12,100	14,900	16,912	17,500	128,112
Operating hours	1,638	1,710	1,490	1,650	1,360	1,575	1,620	1,640	12,683
Operating days	181	180	175	181	160	175	180	181	1,413
Income (£)	14,500	16,289	13,376	16,100	10,285	13,410	15,400	15,900	115,260
Expenditure									
	£	£	£	£	£	£	£	£	£
Road fund licence	75	75	75	75	75	75	75	75	600
Local authority registration	65	65	65	65	65	65	65	65	520
Insurance	610	700	590	620	575	550	610	560	4,815
Maintenance: fixed	60	64	60	77	95	70	85	80	591
variable	60	65	70	68	300	70	75	72	780
Wages	6,500	6,800	5,960	6,600	5,440	6,300	6,480	6,560	50,640
Tyres	80	85	75	85	65	81	87	90	648
Fuel	1,210	1,561	1,220	1,310	875	1,077	1,185	1,310	9,748
Depreciation	1,250	1,050	900	1,000	875	800	1,050	850	7,775
Administration	2,180	2,180	2,180	2,180	2,180	2,180	2,180	2,180	17,440
	12,090	12,645	11,195	12,080	10,545	11,268	11,892	11,842	93,557
Profit/(loss)	2,410	3,644	2,181	4,020	(260)	2,142	3,508	4,058	21,703

Variable costs comprise: fuel, wages, tyres plus variable maintenance costs.

Fixed costs comprise: road fund licence, Local Authority Registration fee, insurance, depreciation, administration plus fixed maintenance costs.

Contribution = income – variable costs.

MONTHLY ANALYSIS OF INCOME AND EXPENDITURE

	Income £	Expenditure £
January	18,894	15,310
February	18,405	15,425
March	18,820	14,875
April	18,774	17,322
May	19,942	14,285
June 20X7	20,425	16,340
-	115,260	93,557

Practice activity 4

Prepare the following key financial ratios for each vehicle and for the business overall for the six months ended 30 June 20X7. Calculate the ratios to the nearest penny, or in the case of percentages, to one decimal place.

(a)　Income per operating mile

(b)　Income per operating hour

6

(c)   Income per operating day
(d)   Contribution per operating mile
(e)   Contribution per operating hour
(f)   Contribution per operating day
(g)   Variable costs per operating mile
(h)   Variable costs per operating hour
(i)   Variable costs per operating day
(j)   Fixed costs per operating mile
(k)   Fixed costs per operating hour
(l)   Fixed costs per operating day
(m)   Net profit (loss) per operating mile
(n)   Net profit (loss) per operating hour
(o)   Net profit (loss) per operating day
(p)   Percentage net profit to income

Practice activity 5

Prepare an appropriate graph or chart showing the analysis of total turnover for the period into variable costs, fixed costs and net profit. You are not required to show the results for individual vehicles on the graph or chart.

Practice activity 6

Prepare a table showing the performance ranking of the vehicles on the basis of net profit/(loss) per operating day.

Practice activity 7

The owner of Emerald Taxis is planning to add a further vehicle to his fleet of cars. He anticipates that the new vehicle will operate for 36,500 miles per annum.

Prepare a statement to estimate the annual income and costs for the new vehicle using, as a basis, the average of your figures for the key indicators you have prepared for the six months ended 30 June 20X7 (answer to Practice activity 4).

Assume that the fixed costs for the vehicle are the same as the average fixed costs for the current vehicles.

Practice activity 8

Over the past five years the annual income of Emerald Taxis has been as follows.

	£
20X2	153,640
20X3	167,040
20X4	185,600
20X5	201,000
20X6	215,000

The RPI for the period 20X2-20X6 was as follows.

20X2	139.2
20X3	141.9
20X4	146.0
20X5	150.7
20X6	155.1

Convert the figures to real terms based on 20X6. Include the real annual year-on-year growth in turnover in your analysis.

Practice activity 9

Using your answer to Practice activity 8, present the actual and real terms income figures for the period 20X2 to 20X6 in the form of a clearly labelled compound bar chart.

Practice activity 10

Complete the form below.

NATIONAL TAXI FEDERATION
RETURN FOR SIX MONTHS ENDED 30 JUNE 20X7

Company name: Emerald Taxis Limited
Membership number: EM002

Performance statistics:		*This period*	*20X6 full year*	*NTF 20X6 average*
Average revenue per vehicle operating day	....		£78.02	£79.70
Average total costs per vehicle operating day	....		£61.07	£60.14
Average revenue per operating mile	....		£0.88	£0.87
Average total costs per operating mile	....		£0.68	£0.67
Net profit as percentage of total revenue	....		17.1%	22.9%
Average mileage per operating day	....		88.66 miles	91.84 miles
Average mileage per operating hour	....		10.01 miles	9.75 miles

Signed: _____ Date: _____

Please submit this form to NTF Head Office as soon as possible.

Practice activity 11

The following table shows details of Penny Farthing Ltd's employees from 1 December 20X7 to 30 June 20X7.

Summary of employees who were employed by Penny Farthing Ltd during the six months to 30 June 20X7

Employee's initials	Age	Male/female	Full/part time	Date of joining/leaving
ARB	27	M	F	Joined 18.11.X5
NC	34	F	F	Joined 1.11.X6
ROD	37	M	P	Joined 1.3.X2; left 31.5.X7
RJ	47	M	P	Joined 20.1.X7
ALK	26	F	F	Joined 1.10.X6
PRM	38	M	P	Joined 24.8.X1
IP	34	M	P	Joined 29.9.X4
JJS	49	M	P	Joined 12.4.X3
RT	41	M	F	Joined 12.8.X6
FWT	36	M	F	Joined 2.1.X7
SRW	29	F	F	Joined 5.3.X7
TW	35	F	F	Joined 15.5.X5; left 20.3.X7
VAW	27	F	P	Joined 1.4.X6; left 15.4.X7

Complete Sections 2 and 4 of the following form from the Office for National Statistics.

A compulsory inquiry conducted by

the Government Statistical Service
IN CONFIDENCE

Office for National Statistics
Newport, Gwent NP9 1XG

Office for National Statistics

Penny Farthing Ltd
14 Church Street
Swindon
Wiltshire
SN21 7QZ

Our ref TI5/404140000 96/941
Please give this reference number if you contact us

Please correct any errors in name, address or postcode
Inquiries into turnover of transport businesses

SECOND QUARTER 20X7 (1 APRIL 20X7 TO 30 JUNE 20X7)

Notice under Section 1 of the Statistics of Trade Act 1947

Dear Contributor

Every quarter we send out this inquiry to obtain up-to-date statistics about transport businesses. All larger businesses and a sample of smaller ones are included. Your business has been included in the inquiry.

Your figures will be used with those from other businesses to provide government with information about developments in your sector and in the economy. Together with other information, this is an essential part of economic forecasting and policy making.

The inquiry results contribute to quarterly estimates of Gross Domestic Product which are published in an ONS press notice and in other ONS publications.

Because of the importance of the information, this is a statutory inquiry. *Under the Act of 1947, it is compulsory for you to provide the information. This should be returned within three weeks of the end of the period which it covers.* The information you provide will be treated as strictly confidential as required by the Act. I can assure you that it will not be revealed in published statistics in a way which would allow anybody to identify your business or be given to any unauthorised person without your permission.

To save you time, we have made the form as short as possible. There are notes to help you but if you have any difficulties or need more information, my staff on the telephone number shown above will be pleased to assist. If exact figures are not available, informed estimates will do. If you need additional copies of the form, please let us know.

Please accept my thanks for your co-operation. Without this we could not provide a good service to government.

Yours sincerely,

Official use only	
Rec only	
Receipted	
Data pre T/O	
On line TO	
P/A	

Business Statistics Division

IMPORTANT

Please read the notes before you fill in this form. Give the best estimates you can if you do not have exact figures.

FV			
T15/4 0414000096/941			

1. Details of business

Your business is classified as being in the industry described briefly in the letter accompanying this form. If you think this is wrong, please give a full description of your business. If you are involved in two or more activities, please describe the main one.

2. Period

Period for which you have filled in the form

		Day	Month	Year	
from		/	/		1
					1
to		/	/		1
					2

3. Turnover to the nearest £thousand (not including VAT)
Total turnover (including fees receivable)

	40

4. Employees

Number of persons employed by the business at the end of the period covered by this return.

4.1	Total employees	50

of which

4.2	Full-time male	51
4.3	Part-time male	52
4.4	Full-time female	53
4.5	Part-time female	54

5. Other businesses included in this form

The form should be completed for the business named in the covering letter. If, exceptionally, you are unable to limit your return to the activities of this business, please list below the names and VAT registration numbers of the other businesses included.

Name of business	VAT registration number
....	....
....	....

(Please continue on a separate sheet if necessary)

REMARKS: If you have given any information which is significantly different from the last quarter, please explain.

....
....

PLEASE USE BLOCK CAPITALS

Name of person we should contact if necessary:

Position in business: Date:

Telephone no./ext: Fax/Telex:

NOTES ON FILLING IN THIS FORM

Quarterly inquiries into turnover

Period

Your return should cover the three months shown on the front of the form. If you do not have figures for that period, the return may be made for the nearest period of a similar length as long as it relates mainly to the one specified. It is important that there are no gaps or overlaps with this period and the period covered by any previous returns that you have made to this inquiry.

Turnover

Give the total amount receivable by the business for services provided or goods sold during the period covered by the form. These amounts should not include VAT. Do not include any amounts receivable from selling or transferring capital assets. The figure given should be for services or goods which you have invoiced rather than cash which you have received, unless a figure for invoiced amounts is not readily available. It is important that the figure is given on a consistent basis from quarter to quarter. Show it to the nearest £ thousand. For example £27,025 should be shown as 27.

Scope of the inquiry

Your turnover should include any business activities carried out within the United Kingdom, (that is England, Scotland, Wales and Northern Ireland). This should include work done in connection with overseas contracts or activities for which invoices are issued by you in the United Kingdom.

Employees

Include full-time and part-time employees (part-time means those who normally work 30 hours a week or less); temporary and casual workers; those off sick, on holiday or on short-term; youth training scheme trainees who have a contract of employment and employment trainees on continuation training; employees who work away from the workplace such as sales reps and lorry drivers.

Exclude those employed by outside contractors or agencies, working proprietors, partners, self-employed, directors not on contract; youth training scheme or employment training trainees without a contract of employment; home workers on piecework rates; former employees still on payroll as pensioners; those who normally work at another establishment such as temporary transfers and secondments.

BPP
PUBLISHING

The following data is required for Practice activities 12-15.

RAYTONBANK FOODS LTD

FINANCIAL RESULTS FOR THE SIX MONTHS TO JUNE 20X7

Store	Whitby	Scarboro	Stokesley	Guisboro	York	Thirsk	Malton	Total
Total sales area (sq ft)	11,000	12,500	9,700	9,500	13,500	9,800	8,750	74,750
Full-time equivalent employees (June)	55	60	45	45	60	40	40	345
	£'000	£'000	£'000	£'000	£'000	£'000	£'000	£'000
Turnover	3,871	4,309	3,212	3,188	4,253	2,817	2,400	24,050
Operating expenses	3,633	4,051	3,022	2,999	3,989	2,650	2,270	22,614
Net profit	238	258	190	189	264	167	130	1,436
Operating expenses include:								
Wages and salaries	341	380	272	271	379	250	250	2,143
Depreciation	25	28	22	22	31	23	19	170
Bought out items, goods and services	3,267	3,643	2,728	2,706	3,579	2,377	2,001	20,301

The weekly sales figures for the six months to June 20X7 are as follows.

(*Note*. The weekly periods for which sales statistics are collected do not correspond with the ends of months. For accounting purposes, the company treats the end of the month as falling on the Saturday closest to the end of the calendar month.)

Accounting month ending Saturday	Sales £	Number of weeks
1 February	4,625,810	5
1 March	3,808,701	4
29 March	3,698,125	4
3 May	4,494,205	5
31 May	3,774,887	4
28 June 20X7	3,648,221	4

An analysis of the company's employees at the beginning and end of the six months to June 20X7 shows the following.

	Number employed		Full-time equivalent	
	29.12.X6	28.6.X7	29.12.X6	28.6.X7
Full-time male	116	110	116	110
Full-time female	188	190	188	190
Part-time male	27	25	13	12
Part-time female	71	75	31	33
	402	400	348	345

Practice activity 12

Prepare the following key performance ratios and other statistics for Raytonbank Foods Ltd for the six month period to June 20X7, for each store and for the business as a whole.

1   Turnover per employee
2   Net profit per employee
3   Sales per square foot
4   Wages and salaries per employee
5   Value added per employee
6   Value added per £1 of employee costs
7   % net profit to sales

NB. Value added is defined as Turnover *less* Bought out items, goods and services.

Employee costs comprise wages and salaries.

In calculating these ratios, use full-time equivalents for employee numbers.

Practice activity 13

The following UK average grocery retail productivity measures are available. 'Employee' for these purposes means 'full-time equivalent employee'.

	£
Annual turnover per employee	140,842
Annual net profit per employee	8,752
Annual wages/salaries per employee	13,941
Weekly sales per sq ft of sales area	17.0
	0

Prepare a table comparing the above productivity measures for Raytonbank Foods Ltd for the six months to June 20X7 with the UK average productivity measures.

Practice activity 14

The relationship of net profit to turnover as a percentage in this type of business is typically low. Grocery retail businesses generally combine high sales volume with a low profit margin.

Using the figures for Raytonbank Foods Ltd for the six months to June 20X7, present a component bar chart to show how overall turnover is related to the different categories of operating expenses and net profit.

Practice activity 15

Starting on Sunday 29 June 20X7, the stores in Stokesley, Guisborough, Thirsk and Malton began opening on Sundays as part of an experiment.

Sales figures for the stores in the 5-week accounting month of July 20X7 are as follows.

		Wh	*Sc*	*St*	*Gu*	*Yo*	*Th*	*Ma*
Week ending		£'000	£'000	£'000	£'000	£'000	£'000	£'000
5 July	Sun	-	-	20	24	-	17	15
	Mon - Sat	147	167	120	117	166	93	80
12 July	Sun	-	-	19	22	-	14	20
	Mon - Sat	158	159	122	120	172	94	84
19 July	Sun	-	-	16	19	-	14	20
	Mon - Sat	159	182	127	123	176	99	87
26 July	Sun	-	-	14	18	-	13	14
	Mon - Sat	161	177	126	122	175	96	76

Prepare a *table* showing the percentage change in average weekly turnover for each store for July compared with each store's average weekly turnover in the half year before the start of Sunday opening. In the table, group together:

(a) those stores which have begun Sunday opening; and
(b) those which have not.

Practice activities

Practice activity 16

Sales growth for Cloverdale Ltd over the past five years has been as follows.

Turnover	£m
20X2	33.7
20X3	37.2
20X4	40.1
20X5	42.3
20X6	44.1

The Retail Prices Index for these years was as follows.

20X2	139.2
20X3	141.9
20X4	146.0
20X5	150.7
20X6	155.1

Convert the figures to real terms based on 20X6, and to show the real annual year-on-year growth in turnover.

The following data relate to Practice activities 17-25

As the accounts clerk at Tonk plc, you have been supplied with the following documents from which to prepare the company's VAT account and VAT return for the three months ended 30 November 20X7. Assume that no further documents will be issued in connection with any of these transactions. You are warned that some invoices contain errors (which you can detect).

TONK PLC
1 Plink Lane, Infertown. IN2 4DA
VAT reg no 154 9131 32

Invoice no. 572
Date: 4 September 20X7
Tax point: 4 September 20X7

To: Bar plc

32 Stoke Street
London NW12

	VAT rate	£
	%	
Sales of goods		
3,000 small suitcases	17.5	33,750.00
4,500 handbags	17.5	15,840.00
Total excluding VAT		49,590.00
Total VAT at 17.5%		8,504.68
Total payable within 30 days		58,094.68
Less 2% discount if paid within 10 days		991.80
Total payable within 10 days		57,102.88

TONK PLC
1 Plink Lane, Infertown. IN2 4DA
VAT reg no 154 9131 32

Invoice no. 573

Date: 12 September 20X7
Tax point: 12 September 20X7

To: Cormick Ltd

      63 Saddle Road
      Gulltown GL4 3CE

	VAT rate	
	%	£
Sales of goods		
2,000 trunks	17.5	38,000.00
7,000 shopping bags	17.5	14,000.00
Total excluding VAT		52,000.00
Total VAT at 17.5%		10,400.00
Total payable within 30 days, strictly net		62,400.00

TONK PLC

1 Plink Lane, Infertown. IN2 4DA
VAT reg no 154 9131 32

Invoice no. 574
Date: 3 October 20X7
Tax point: 3 October 20X7

To: Work plc

      99 Mark Lane
      Cartown CA1 9TP

	VAT rate	
	%	£
Sales of goods		
7,200 large suitcases	17.5	106,992.00
6,350 handbags	17.5	22,352.00
		129,344.00
Less 5% quantity discount		6,467.20
Total excluding VAT		122,876.80
Total VAT at 17.5%		18,431.52
Total payable within 30 days, strictly net		141,308.32

TONK PLC

1 Plink Lane, Infertown. IN2 4DA
VAT reg no 154 9131 32

Invoice no. 575
Date: 12 November 20X7
Tax point: 12 November 20X7

To: Monet plc

       39 Giro Street
       Bingotown BN6 2BC

	VAT rate %	£
Sales of goods		
7,000 small suitcases	17.5	78,750.00
10,000 briefcases	17.5	158,700.00
Total excluding VAT		237,450.00
Total VAT at 17.5%		40,722.67
Total payable within 30 days		278,172.67
Less 2% discount if paid within 10 days		4,749.00
Total payable within 10 days		273,423.67

TONK PLC

1 Plink Lane, Infertown. IN2 4DA
VAT reg no 154 9131 32

Credit note no. 34
Date: 3 November 20X7
Tax point: 3 November 20X7

To: Sole plc

       14 Power Street
       Abbatown AB4 3BZ

Credit in respect of returned defective goods (invoice number 520; invoice date 1 July 20X7)

	VAT rate %	£
125 handbags	17.5	440.00
VAT at 17.5%		77.00
Total credit		517.00

TONK PLC
MEMORANDUM

To: Accounts clerk
From: Credit controller
Date: 2 October 20X7

Please write off the following two debts.

Debtor	Date payment due	Net	VAT	Gross
		£	£	£
Off Ltd	1.8.X7	2,000	350	2,350
Trib Ltd	14.1.X7	3,800	665	4,465

TONK PLC

MEMORANDUM

To: Accounts clerk
From: Finance director
Date: 4 November 20X7

Our auditors have found errors in our VAT accounting in a previous period. Output VAT was overstated by £2,500, and input VAT was overstated by £1,600. Please take the necessary corrective action.

TARSKI PLC

VAT reg no 110 2511 35   79 Reff Road
Date: 12 October 20X7   Selltown
Tax point: 12 October 20X7   SL2 9AT
Invoice no. 88577
To: Tonk plc
          1 Plink Lane
          Infertown IN2 4DA

	Net	VAT rate	VAT
	£	%	£
Sales of goods			
10,000 small suitcases	60,000.00	17.5	10,500.00
10,000 large suitcases	80,000.00	17.5	14,000.00
4,200 briefcases	30,660.00	17.5	5,365.50
Total excluding VAT	170,660.00		29,865.50
Total VAT at 17.5%	29,865.50		
Total payable within 30 days	200,525.50		

COURSE LTD

35 Work Street, Infertown IN3 7ET
VAT reg no 624 0668 24

15 October 20X7

Sale of 2,000 steel corner brackets: £83.60 including VAT at 17.5%.

SILK LTD

74 Hull Street, Infertown IN1 5DD
VAT reg no 281 8238 13

Date of supply

This is a less detailed invoice for VAT purposes.

Sale of 3,500 brass clips: £270.25 including VAT at 17.5%.

TARSKI PLC
79 Reff Road
Selltown
SL2 9AT

VAT reg no 110 2511 35
Date: 5 November 20X7
Credit note no. 324
To: Tonk plc
        1 Plink Lane
        Infertown IN2 4DA

CREDIT NOTE

(Invoice no. 88577, date 12 October 20X7)

	£
200 defective small suitcases returned	1,200.00
VAT at 17.5%	210.00
Gross credit	1,410.00

TONK PLC

EXPENSES CLAIM

Name: A Spender   Three months ended: 30.11.X7

	Net	VAT	Gross
	£	£	£
Business entertaining			
(VAT invoice attached)	300.00	52.50	352.50
Call from public telephone*	5.11	0.89	6.00
Car park fee*	15.32	2.68	18.00
Car park fee*	25.54	4.46	30.00
	345.97	60.53	406.50

* No invoice or receipt issued

Authorised: A Manager

Practice activity 17

Outline the errors which you have detected in the documents supplied to you.

Practice activities 18-25 are to be completed assuming invoices corrected for the above errors have been reissued by Tonk plc.

Practice activity 18

Calculate Tonk plc's output VAT for the 3 months ended 30 November 20X7.

Practice activity 19

Calculate Tonk plc's input VAT for the 3 months ended 30 November 20X7.

Practice activity 20

Calculate Tonk plc's total net turnover for the 3 months ended 30 November 20X7.

Practice activity 21

Calculate Tonk plc's total net purchases for the 3 months ended 30 November 20X7.

Practice activity 22

What is the net error relating to the previous VAT accounting period? How is it accounted for?

Practice activity 23

Prepare the VAT account for the VAT period from September to November 20X7.

Practice activity 24

Prepare Tonk plc's VAT return for the 3 months ended 30 November 20X7 (using the results from Activity 22). A blank VAT return is provided below.

Value Added Tax Return
For the period
01 09 X7 to 30 11 X7

For Official Use

Registration number | Period

154 9131 32 | 11 X7

You could be liable to a financial penalty if your completed return and all the VAT payable are not received by the due date.

TONK PLC
1 PLINK LANE
INFERTOWN
IN2 4DA

Due date: 31 12 X7

For Official Use

Your VAT Office telephone number is 0123-4567

Before you fill in this form please read the notes on the back and the VAT Leaflet *"Filling in your VAT return"*. Fill in all boxes clearly in ink, and write 'none' where necessary. Don't put a dash or leave any box blank. If there are no pence write "00" in the pence column. Do not enter more than one amount in any box.

For official use			£	p
VAT due in this period on sales and other outputs	1			
VAT due in this period on acquisitions from other EC Member States	2			
Total VAT due (the sum of boxes 1 and 2)	3			
VAT reclaimed in this period on purchases and other inputs (including acquisitions from the EC)	4			
Net VAT to be paid to Customs or reclaimed by you (Difference between boxes 3 and 4)	5			
Total value of sales and all other outputs excluding any VAT. Include your box 8 figure	6			00
Total value of purchases and all other inputs excluding any VAT. Include your box 9 figure	7			00
Total value of all supplies of goods and related services, excluding any VAT, to other EC Member States	8			00
Total value of all acquisitions of goods and related services, excluding any VAT, from other EC Member States	9			00

Retail schemes. If you have used any of the schemes in the period covered by this return, enter the relevant letter(s) in this box.

DECLARATION: You, or someone on your behalf, must sign below.

If you are enclosing a payment please tick this box.

I, ... declare that the
(Full name of signatory in BLOCK LETTERS)
information given above is true and complete.

Signature.. Date .... 20 ....
A false declaration can result in prosecution.

Practice activity 25

State the date on which the VAT return is due to be received by Customs & Excise and on which date the overall VAT due will be paid to Customs.

The following information relates to Practice activities 26-35.

The following documents relate to Strode Ltd for the three months ended 30 June 20X3. All transactions were with persons in the United Kingdom.

SUMMARY OF SUPPLIES MADE			
(Some columns not shown)			
Date	*Item*	*VAT rate*	*Net amount*
		%	£
2.4.X3	Stockbroking services	Exempt	62,000
12.4.X3	Sale of books about finance	0.0	27,000
21.4.X3	Stockbroking services	Exempt	35,250
30.4.X3	Stockbroking services	Exempt	24,870
2.5.X3	Sale of books about finance	0.0	33,500
12.5.X3	Investment advice	17.5	3,850
28.5.X3	Trust administration services	17.5	11,250
4.6.X3	Sale of books	0.0	7,500
10.6.X3	Investment advice	17.5	8,500
17.6.X3	Insurance broking services for a UK company	Exempt	1,800
30.6.X3	Stockbroking services	Exempt	32,000

SUMMARY OF SUPPLIES RECEIVED			
(Some columns not shown)			
Date	*Item*	*VAT rate*	*Net amount*
		%	£
1.4.X3	New car for managing director	17.5	15,000
12.4.X3	Petrol	17.5	600
2.5.X3	Office furniture	17.5	5,400
3.6.X3	Stationery	17.5	7,400
15.6.X3	Computer bureau services	17.5	22,000
17.6.X3	Materials to make own stationery	17.5	3,000

MEMORANDUM	
To:	Accountant
From:	Finance director
Date:	10 July 20X3
Subject:	Your memo of 6 July 20X3

Thank you for your enquiries. I can reply as follows.

(a) The managing director was supplied with fuel free of charge for both business and private use. The car has a 1,800 cc petrol engine. The scale charge per quarter is £325.

(b) I agree that in the tax period ended 31 March 20X3 the company's output VAT was understated by £870.

MEMORANDUM

To: Accountant
From: Stationery department
Date: 7 July 20X3
Subject: Internal production of stationery

In June, in addition to our purchase of stationery, we produced our own stationery, at a cost (including materials (£3,000 before VAT), wages and production overhead) of £16,000. This is about the average quarterly cost of such production. All costs exclude any VAT.

MEMORANDUM

To: Accountant
From: Assistant accountant
Date: 18 July 20X3
Subject: Supplies received and supplies made

I have established that the only supply received which can be attributed to particular supplies made is the computer bureau services, which are entirely attributable to stockbroking. The stationery which we produced for our own use was not attributable to any particular supplies.

MEMORANDUM

To: Accountant
From: Credit controller
Date: 17 June 20X3
Subject: Bad debts

One of our clients, A Jones, to whom we have supplied only investment advice, now seems unlikely to pay his outstanding debts to us, so these debts should be written off. A complete list of supplies to this client is as follows.

Due date for payment of debt	Amount including VAT
	£
1.3.X2	724
1.12.X2	830
1.3.X3	680
31.3.X3	520
10.6.X3	327

A Jones paid £1,000 on 15 December 20X2 and £200 on 1 January 20X3 but did not specify which invoices the payments were in respect of.

Practice activity 26

Calculate the VAT on supplies made in the 3 months ended 30 June 20X3.

Practice activity 27

Calculate the VAT on supplies received for the 3 months ended 30 June 20X3.

Practice activity 28

Calculate the VAT on the fuel for private use.

Practice activity 29

How is the understatement of output VAT for the previous 3 month period accounted for?

Practice activity 30

How is the internal production of stationery accounted for (in terms of VAT)?

Practice activity 31

How much VAT can be claimed immediately under bad debt relief? When can the remaining VAT be claimed?

Practice activity 32

What is Strode Ltd's recoverable input VAT for the 3 months ended 30 June 20X3?

Practice activity 33

What is Strode Ltd's output VAT for the 3 months ended 30 June 20X3?

Practice activity 34

Prepare Strode Ltd's VAT return for the period from 1 April to 30 June 20X3. A blank VAT return is provided below.

Value Added Tax Return

For the period
01 03 X3 to 30 06 X3

For Official Use

Registration number | Period
431 9824 79 | 06 X3

You could be liable to a financial penalty
if your completed return and all the VAT
payable are not received by the due date.

Due date: 31 07 X3

For Official Use

STRODE LTD
63 FIG STREET
TREETOWN
TR14NF

Your VAT Office telephone number is 0123-4567

Before you fill in this form please read the notes on the back and the VAT Leaflet *"Filling in your VAT return"*.
Complete all boxes clearly in ink, and write 'none' where necessary. Don't put a dash or leave any box blank. If there are no pence
write "00" in the pence column. Do not enter more than one amount in any box.

For official use		£	p
	VAT due in this period on sales and other outputs **1**		
	VAT due in this period on acquisitions from other EC Member States **2**		
	Total VAT due (the sum of boxes 1 and 2) **3**		
	VAT reclaimed in this period on purchases and other inputs (including acquisitions from the EC) **4**		
	Net VAT to be paid to Customs or reclaimed by you (Difference between boxes 3 and 4) **5**		
	Total value of sales and all other outputs excluding any VAT. Include your box 8 figure **6**		00
	Total value of purchases and all other inputs excluding any VAT. Include your box 9 figure **7**		00
	Total value of all supplies of goods and related services, excluding any VAT, to other EC Member States **8**		00
	Total value of all acquisitions of goods and related services, excluding any VAT, from other EC Member States **9**		00

Retail schemes. If you have used any of the schemes in the period covered by this return, enter the relevant letter(s) in this box.

If you are enclosing a payment please tick this box.	DECLARATION: You, or someone on your behalf, must sign below.
	I, ... declare that the
	(Full name of signatory in BLOCK LETTERS)
	information given above is true and complete.
	Signature.. Date 20
	A false declaration can result in prosecution.

Practice activity 35

State how you would justify your claim for bad debt relief if it were to be challenged by HM Customs & Excise.

BPP PUBLISHING

Practice Devolved Assessments

Practice Devolved Assessment
1 Grady's Tutorial College

Performance criteria

The following performance criteria are covered in this Practice Devolved Assessment.

Element 7.1: Prepare and present periodic performance reports

1   Information derived from different units of the organisation is consolidated into the appropriate form.

2   Information derived from different information systems within the organisation is correctly reconciled.

3   When comparing results over time an appropriate method which allows for changing price levels is used.

4   Transactions between separate units of the organisation are accounted for in accordance with the organisation's procedures.

5   Ratios and performance indicators are accurately calculated in accordance with the organisation's procedures.

6   Reports are prepared in the appropriate form and presented to management within required timescales.

Element 7.2: Prepare reports and returns for outside agencies

1   Relevant information is identified, collated and presented in accordance with the conventions and definitions used by outside agencies.

2   Calculations of ratios and performance indicators are accurate.

3   Authorisation for the despatch of completed reports and returns is sought from the appropriate person.

4   Reports and returns are presented in accordance with outside agencies' requirements and deadlines.

Instructions

This Assessment is designed to test your ability to prepare and present periodic performance reports and to prepare returns for outside agencies.

You are provided with data on the situation which you must use to complete the tasks listed. You are advised to read through the whole of the Assessment before commencing as all of the information may be of value and is not necessarily supplied in the sequence in which you might wish to deal with it. Part of your answer will require filling in a form on pages 31-35. You should complete the other tasks using your own paper.

You are allowed 2½ hours to complete your work.

A high level of accuracy is required. Check your work carefully. Correcting fluid may be used but should be used in moderation. Errors should be crossed out neatly and clearly. You should write in black ink, not pencil. Do not use any additional notes or books during this Practice Devolved Assessment. **A full answer to this Assessment is provided on page 127**. Do not turn to the suggested answer until you have completed all parts of the Assessment.

Data

You are employed on a temporary assignment at Grady's Tutorial College. The College was set up in 20W8 and provides training courses, particularly for those wishing to return to work after a career break. Since 20X0, the college has also operated a small bookshop which sells mainly to course registrants but also to members of the public.

It is 12 April 20X4. Kim Harvey, the Financial Controller, hands to you some Office for National Statistics forms (see pages 29 to 34) which she received some time ago. At 5.30pm today, Kim, who needs to authorise the form, is leaving to go on a 10-day holiday. She asks if you would make sure that the forms are available for her to sign on her return from holiday.

Kim's telephone number at the college is 020-7711 4240 (Fax: 020-7711 4200).

The business has two divisions, called College Division (courses) and Bookshop (book sales). The accounting year end is 31 March.

The following table shows 'year-to-date' (YTD) figures for the business as at the end of each quarter in the year ending 31 March 20X4. These figures have been extracted from management accounts.

	30 June 20X3 YTD £	*30 Sept 20X3* YTD £	*31 Dec 20X3* YTD £	*31 March 20X4* YTD £
College Division				
Turnover	124,694	269,818	422,629	583,636
Direct costs	64,128	130,813	199,207	270,010
Other operating costs	22,031	43,498	72,882	97,509
Bookshop				
Turnover	12,721	28,223	46,931	71,094
Cost of sales	8,081	17,710	29,614	44,829
Staff costs	4,211	8,321	12,600	17,014
Other operating costs	2,412	4,401	6,589	9,420

Bookshop turnover includes books removed from the shop by members of College Division for their own use in course teaching. These books are invoiced at the full cover price to College Division, which has included them in 'other operating costs'. The average mark-up on the cost of books is 35%. The amounts of such interdivisional sales were as follows in the year to March 20X4.

Interdivisional book sales (at cover price): Year to March 20X4

Month	£	Month	£
Apr	205	Oct	234
May	110	Nov	121
Jun	20	Dec	333
Jul	312	Jan	394
Aug	333	Feb	481
Sep	214	Mar	192

Staff

College Division has employed 10 full-time members of staff (6 women and 4 men) and 1 part-time male member of staff throughout the whole of the year to 31 March 20X4. In the same year, the bookshop has employed 1 full-time male staff member and 1 part-time female staff member, who started her job at the beginning of July 20X3.

Fixed assets

The following information has been extracted from the fixed asset register of Grady's Tutorial College.

	Land and buildings £	Plant and machinery £	Motor vehicles £	Office equipment £	Total £
Cost					
At 1 January 20X4	154,500	9,840	27,900	10,240	202,480
Additions	56,250	2,840	9,890	1,280	70,260
Disposals	-	(4,465)	(14,700)	(2,980)	(22,145)
At 31 March 20X4	210,750	8,215	23,090	8,540	250,595
Depreciation					
At 1 January 20X4	-	6,720	19,220	5,745	31,685
Charge for quarter	-	355	1,720	540	2,615
Disposals	-	(3,465)	(10,200)	(940)	(14,605)
At 31 March 20X4	-	3,610	10,740	5,345	19,695

Of the additions to land and buildings shown above, £32,150 was spent in buying a small building adjacent to the college. The remainder of these additions was in respect of improvements to the building in order to convert it to lecture room accommodation.

Certain fixed assets were sold, all for cash, in the quarter to 31 March 20X4. The debit entries in the cash book in respect of these sales are summarised below.

	£
Land and buildings	-
Plant and machinery	1,400
Motor vehicles	5,200
Office equipment	1,655

Tasks

(a) Complete the Office for National Statistics forms in accordance with the accompanying notes (see pages 89 to 94).

(b) State how much time is available for the ONS forms to be completed. State what action you would take to ensure that the forms are submitted on time.

(c) Kim also requires you to set out in a table various items of information specified below for the following four periods.
   (i) Quarter ending 30 June 20X3
   (ii) Quarter ending 30 September 20X3
   (iii) Quarter ending 31 December 20X3
   (iv) Quarter ending 31 March 20X4

The information required is as follows. (Design your table with care before you begin this task.)

College Division
Turnover*
Direct costs*
Other operating costs*
Contribution*
Direct costs as % of turnover
Other operating costs as % of turnover
Contribution as % of turnover

* in £'000 to one decimal place

Notes. Contribution = Turnover – (Direct costs + Other operating costs)

BPP
PUBLISHING

Bookshop
Turnover (including sales to College Division)
Cost of sales★
Staff costs★
Other operating costs★
Gross profit★
Contribution★
Gross profit percentage (ie as % of turnover)
Sales per staff member
Contribution as % of turnover

★ in £'000 to one decimal place

Notes. Gross profit = Turnover – Cost of sales
Contribution = Gross profit – (Staff costs + Other operating costs)

For the purpose of calculating numbers of staff members in this task, a part-time staff member is treated as equivalent to one half of a full-time member of staff.

(d) Present the following ratios and percentages for each of the four quarters to 31 March 20X4, as calculated in Task (c) above, in an appropriate graphical format.

(i) College Division:
Direct costs as % of turnover
Other operating costs as % of turnover
Contribution as % of turnover

(ii) Bookshop:
Gross profit percentage
Sales per staff member

(e) An issue raised at a management meeting has been that of whether it is possible to measure the productivity of the teaching staff at Grady's Tutorial College. This has proved to be a contentious matter. You have been invited to attend the next management meeting to make a contribution to this discussion.

In preparation for the meeting, outline briefly different ways in which the productivity of the teaching staff might be measured, indicating the records which you consider would be necessary if such measurement is to be possible.

All calculations are to be displayed to two places of decimals.

Tutorial note. The fictitious letter below (pages 31 to 33) includes a Notice under Section 1 of the Statistics of Trade Act 1947 of a type sent out by the Office for National Statistics (ONS).

A compulsory inquiry conducted by
the Government Statistical Service
IN CONFIDENCE

Office for National Statistics

Office for National Statistics
Newport, Gwent NP9 1XG

Grady's Tutorial College
Attn Kim Harvey
Grady House
295 Edgerton Road
London
NW5 7XR

Our ref TI6/7704240000 72/112
Please give this reference number if you contact us

Please correct any errors in name, address or postcode   **26 March 20X4**

Quarterly inquiries into turnover of the distributive and service trades

FIRST QUARTER 20X4 (1 JAN 20X4 TO 31 MARCH 20X4)

Notice under Section 1 of the Statistics of Trade Act 1947

Dear Contributor

Every quarter we send out this inquiry to obtain up-to-date statistics about the distributive and service trades. All larger businesses and a sample of smaller ones are included. Your business has been included in the inquiry.

Your figures will be used with those from other businesses to provide government with information about developments in the distributive and service trades and in the economy. Together with other information, this is an essential part of economic forecasting and policy making.

The inquiry results contribute to quarterly estimates of Gross Domestic Product which are published in an ONS press notice and in other ONS publications.

Because of the importance of the information, this is a statutory inquiry. *Under the Act of 1947, it is compulsory for you to provide the information. This should be returned within three weeks of the end of the period which it covers.* The information you provide will be treated as strictly confidential as required by the Act. I can assure you that it will not be revealed in published statistics in a way which would allow anybody to identify your business or be given to any unauthorised person without your permission.

To save you time, we have made the form as short as possible. There are notes to help you but if you have any difficulties or need more information, my staff on the telephone number shown above will be pleased to assist. If exact figures are not available, informed estimates will do. If you need additional copies of the form, please let us know.

Please accept my thanks for your co-operation. Without this we could not provide a good service to government.

Yours sincerely,

Official use only	
Rec only	
Receipted	
Data pre T/O	
On line T/O	
P/A	

Business Statistics Division

IMPORTANT

Please read the notes before you fill in this form. Give the best estimates you can if you do not have exact figures.

	FV			
	T16/7704240000 72/112			

1. **Details of business**

   Your business is classified as being in the industry described briefly in the letter accompanying this form. If you think this is wrong, please give a full description of your business. If you are involved in two or more activities, please describe the main one.

2. **Period**

   Period for which you have filled in the form   from

	Day	Month	Year	
from	/	/		1
				1
to	/	/		1
				2

3. **Turnover** to the nearest £thousand (not including VAT)
   Total turnover (including fees receivable)

	40

4. **Employees**

   Number of persons employed by the business at the end of the period covered by this return.

   4.1   Total employees

	50

   of which:

   4.2   Full-time male

   4.3   Part-time male

   4.4   Full-time female

   4.5   Part-time female

	51
	52
	53
	54

5. **Other businesses included in this form**

   The form should be completed for the business named in the covering letter. If, exceptionally, you are unable to limit your return to the activities of this business, please list below the names and VAT registration numbers of the other businesses included.

   Name of business   VAT registration number

   ....

   ....

   (Please continue on a separate sheet if necessary)

   REMARKS: If you have given any information which is significantly different from the last quarter, please explain.

   ....

   ....

   PLEASE USE BLOCK CAPITALS

   Name of person we should contact if necessary:

   Position in business:

   Telephone no./ext: Fax/Telex: Date:

NOTES ON FILLING IN THIS FORM

Quarterly inquiries into turnover of the distributive and service trades.

Period

Your return should cover the three months shown on the front of the form. If you do not have figures for that period, the return may be made for the nearest period of a similar length as long as it relates mainly to the one specified. It is important that there are no gaps or overlaps with this period and the period covered by any previous returns that you have made to this inquiry.

Turnover

Give the total amount receivable by the business for services provided or goods sold during the period covered by the form. These amounts should not include VAT. Do not include any amounts receivable from selling or transferring capital assets. The figure given should be for services or goods which you have invoiced rather than cash which you have received, unless a figure for invoiced amounts is not readily available. It is important that the figure is given on a consistent basis from quarter to quarter. Show it to the nearest £ thousand. For example £27,025 should be shown as 27.

Scope of the inquiry

Your turnover should include any business activities carried out within the United Kingdom, (that is England, Scotland, Wales and Northern Ireland). This should include work done in connection with overseas contracts or activities for which invoices are issued by you in the United Kingdom.

Employees

Include full-time and part-time employees (part-time means those who normally work 30 hours a week or less); temporary and casual workers; those off sick, on holiday or on short-term; youth training scheme trainees who have a contract of employment and employment trainees on continuation training; employees who work away from the workplace such as sales reps and lorry drivers.

Exclude those employed by outside contractors or agencies, working proprietors, partners, self-employed, directors not on contract; youth training scheme or employment training trainees without a contract of employment; home workers on piecework rates; former employees still on payroll as pensioners; those who normally work at another establishment such as temporary transfers and secondments.

BPP
PUBLISHING

Tutorial note. Like the letter on pages 31 to 33, this fictitious letter (pages 34 to 36) includes an official Notice the same as one used by the ONS. The notes on page 36 do not include all of the notes which the ONS includes with its inquiry form.

Office for National Statistics

A compulsory inquiry conducted by
the Government Statistical Service

IN CONFIDENCE   NEWPORT Gwent NP9 1XG

Ref: QC/17/8100/7104420000/721

GRADY'S TUTORIAL COLLEGE
GRADY HOUSE
249 EDGERTON ROAD
LONDON
NW5 7XR

17 March 20X4

Please correct any errors in name or address

QUARTERLY INQUIRY INTO CAPITAL EXPENDITURE

FIRST QUARTER 20X4 (1 Jan 20X4 to 31 March 20X4)

Notice under Section 1 of the Statistics of Trade Act 1947

Dear Contributor

We conduct this inquiry to obtain up to date information on capital expenditure. The results provide government with essential information for the national accounts and make an important contribution to monitoring the economy. The number of forms is kept to the minimum required to produce reliable results.

Under the above Act, it is necessary for you to provide us with the information requested overleaf. This will be treated as strictly confidential as required by the Act. It will not be revealed in published statistics in a way which would enable your company to be identified, or disclosed to any unauthorised person without your consent.

Please return your completed form by the date shown on the next page of this letter. If exact figures are not readily available, informed estimates are acceptable.

I enclose notes to help you complete the form. In particular, please see the note dealing with the scope of the inquiry. If you have any difficulties in providing data, or on any other point, please contact A.......L...... on 0123 45678.

Thank you for your co-operation.

Yours sincerely

Business Statistics Division
Production Census and Capital Expenditure Branch

PLEASE COMPLETE AND RETURN THIS FORM BY 14 APRIL 20X4

FV	93	Q1
8100/7104420000		

IMPORTANT Please read the enclosed notes before completing this form. If you do not have precise figures available give the best estimates you can. All values should be shown to the nearest £ thousand

1. PERIOD (see note 1

		Day	Month	Year
Period covered by the return	from	08	/	/
09	to	09	/	/

2. LAND AND BUILDINGS (see note 2)   **£ thousand**

2.1 New building work or other constructional work of a capital nature (excluding the cost of land and of new dwellings)	10	
2.2 Acquisition of land and of existing buildings	20	
2.3 Proceeds of land and buildings disposed of	30	

3. VEHICLES (see note 3)

3.1 New and second-hand acquisitions	40	
3.2 Proceeds of vehicles disposed of	50	

4. PLANT, MACHINERY etc (see note 4)

4.1 New and second-hand acquisitions	60	
4.2 Proceeds of plant, machinery etc disposed of	70	

5. TOTAL

5.1 Total acquisitions (2.1 + 2.2 + 3.1 + 4.1)	90	
5.2 Total disposals (2.3 + 3.2 + 4.2)	100	

6. FINANCE LEASING

6.1 Total amount included in acquisitions at 2.1, 3.1 and 4.1 for assets leased under finance leasing arrangements.	80	

7. COMMENTS ON UNUSUAL FLUCTUATIONS IN FIGURES WOULD BE APPRECIATED

....

Name of person to be contacted if necessary...
BLOCK CAPITALS PLEASE

Position in company..................................... Signature...

Telephone No/Ext............................... Fax.......................... Date...........................

Office for National Statistics

NEWPORT Gwent NP9 1XG

QUARTERLY INQUIRY INTO CAPITAL EXPENDITURE
PLEASE READ THESE NOTES BEFORE COMPLETING YOUR RETURN
SCOPE OF THE INQUIRY

This inquiry covers businesses which operate in the United Kingdom. The business is the individual company, partnership, sole proprietorship etc, to which the form has been sent. Figures for subsidiaries of the business addressed should be excluded. In particular, where the business addressed is a holding company figures are required only in respect of the holding company and not for the group as a whole.

NOTES ON INDIVIDUAL QUESTIONS

1.   PERIOD

You should enter the start and end dates of the period covered by your return. This should be the calendar quarter specified on the front of the form, or the nearest period of similar length for which figures are available. Where the period is not the calendar quarter, the start date should be no earlier than 20 November 20X3. The total length of the period should not be less than 12 weeks nor more than 16 weeks.

CAPITAL EXPENDITURE

The amounts entered should generally reflect all acquisitions and disposals charged to capital account during the period, together with any other amounts which are regarded as capital items for taxation purposes.

All figures should exclude valued added tax, except that the non-deductible value added tax and Customs and Excise tax paid on passenger cars should be included. Do not deduct any amounts received in grants and/or allowances from government sources, statutory bodies or local authorities.

Expenditure indirectly associated with the acquisition of capital goods, such as the cost of arranging bank loans and servicing them, should be excluded.

If the capital expenditure of the business is nil or very small, a form should be competed to this effect.

2.   LAND AND BUILDINGS

New building work (2.1)

Include expenditure on the construction of new building works (other than dwellings) contracted by you whether directly with the constructors or arranged via property developers. Also covered here is expenditure on the associated architects' and surveyors' fees and any legal charges, stamp duties, agents' commissions, etc. Any expenditure undertaken by you when acting as a property developer contracted to carry out the building work by a third party should be excluded.

New building work covers the construction of new buildings, and extensions and improvements to old buildings (including fixtures such as lifts, heating and ventilation systems). The cost of site preparation and other civil engineering work should be included but the cost of land should be recorded against question 2.2

Land and existing buildings (2.2 and 2.3)

Against question 2.2 include all expenditure on land and existing buildings. Land purchase in connection with new building work should also be recorded here and should be estimated where precise figures are not known.

Amounts shown should include the capital cost of freeholds and leaseholds purchased and any leasehold premiums paid. Also covered are architect's and surveyor's fees and any legal charges, stamp duties, agent's commissions, etc associated with these transactions.

Under disposals of land and existing buildings (question 2.3) enter the net amount received after deduction of all transfer costs.

3.   VEHICLES (3.1 and 3.2)

These questions cover motor vehicles, ships, aircraft, and railway rolling stock etc.

4.   PLANT, MACHINERY AND OTHER CAPITAL EQUIPMENT (4.1 and 4.2)

These questions cover plant, machinery and all other capital equipment (eg computer equipment, office machinery, furniture, mechanical handling equipment and mobile powered equipment such as earth movers, excavators, levellers, mobile cranes).

Practice Devolved Assessment
2 Iris Ltd

Performance criteria

The following performance criteria are covered in this Practice Devolved Assessment.

Element 7.3: Prepare VAT returns

1   VAT returns are correctly completed using data from the appropriate recording systems and are submitted within the statutory time limits.

2   Relevant inputs and outputs are correctly identified and calculated.

3   Submissions are made in accordance with current legislation.

4   Guidance is sought from the VAT office when required, in a professional manner.

Instructions

This Assessment is designed to test your ability to prepare VAT returns.

You are provided with data (pages 38 to 40) which you must use to complete the tasks listed on page 40.

You are allowed two hours to complete your work.

A high level of accuracy is required. Check your work carefully.

Correcting fluid may be used but should be used in moderation. Errors should be crossed out neatly and clearly. You should write in black ink, not pencil.

A full answer to this Assessment is provided on page 132. Do not turn to the suggested answer until you have completed all parts of the Assessment.

Data

You are the recently appointed accountant at Iris Ltd. You are about to prepare the company's VAT return for the three months ended 31 December 20X5. You have the following documents to help you.

SALES REPORT		
Month	*Sales*	*VAT*
	£	£
October 20X5	327,190.00	40,545.75
November 20X5	458,429.00	63,486.50
December 20X5	259,361.00	31,608.50

PURCHASES REPORT		
Month	*Purchases*	*VAT*
	£	£
October 20X5	210,630.00	22,863.40
November 20X5	296,539.00	32,805.85
December 20X5	137,784.00	16,894.15

MEMORANDUM

To: Accountant
From: Sales Director
Date: 7 January 20X6
Subject: VAT returns

I can provide my usual confirmation that we have done no business (sales or purchases) outside the UK in the quarter just ended and that we have had no dealings in zero rated goods or services. All our exempt sales were of services. All exempt purchases were attributable to exempt sales. 20% of standard rated purchases were attributable to exempt sales, and 45% to standard rated sales.

MEMORANDUM

To: Accountant
From: Warehouse Manager
Date: 13 January 20X6
Subject: Invoicing

I have noticed that in the past month, your department has been working a bit too fast. Goods worth £16,000 (plus VAT) were invoiced before the end of the year, even though they were still in the warehouse when we did our stockcount on 2 January. Won't the customers object to being billed so early? I suppose it's still better for us than the incident three months ago, when goods worth £24,600 (plus VAT) were delivered to the customer on 29 September but not invoiced until 10 October.

MEMORANDUM

To: Accountant
From: Data Processing Manager
Date: 20 January 20X6
Subject: Sales and purchases reports

You telephoned my secretary yesterday and asked a couple of questions about the reports produced by our computerised accounting system. The answers are as follows.

(a)   Sales and purchases are shown net of VAT.

(b)   Any sale of goods is recorded in the system on the day the goods leave the warehouse. This is because we work from the despatch notes. I know that for VAT purposes you always use the date of invoicing, but your predecessor (who left in November) said that she made adjustments on the rare occasions when the invoice did not go out on the same day. We never adjusted our figures to take her adjustments into account. Any sale of services is recorded on the day of invoicing.

MEMORANDUM

To: Accountant
From: Senior Accountant
Date: 23 January 20X6
Subject: VAT treatment of conference costs

A quote for the cost of the Birmingham conference arrived today. The conference, which is basically a vehicle to promote the company's name and products, will be held next month and is a forum for our sales team to meet interested potential customers as well as our suppliers.

The quotation covers room hire, projection equipment hire (to allow promotional films to be shown) and lunch-time food and drink for all delegates. The conference will run from 11am to 4 pm. The VAT element is over £3,000.

Can you draft a letter to HM Customs & Excise asking whether this VAT is recoverable?

MEMORANDUM

To: Accountant
From: Credit Controller
Date: 23 January 20X6
Subject: Bad debts

In March 20X5, we made sales of goods to a customer of £7,600 plus VAT. Payment for the goods was due by 30 April 20X5. We received a cheque for £3,000 in August, but the customer went into liquidation in October. I have now heard that creditors will be paid 40p for every pound they are owed. I have written off the balance of the debt, which will not be paid.

MEMORANDUM

To: Accountant
From: Finance Director
Date: 28 January 20X6
Subject: Mistakes in VAT returns

A friend of mine runs a small business, and he has a query about his VAT. I wouldn't normally trouble you with things which don't concern Iris Ltd directly, but it's probably very simple so I hope you won't mind answering it. He isn't very good at accounts, and is very concerned that he might put the wrong figures on his VAT returns. He wants to know:

(a)   can he just put right any underpayment or overpayment on a later return;

(b)   could he be made to pay a penalty if he makes a mistake?

MEMORANDUM

To: Accountant
From: Data Processing Manager
Date: 28 January 20X6
Subject: New accounting software

We may soon be changing our software. One issue which has come up is that of rounding . The computer could work out amounts of VAT to the nearest hundreth of a penny, but all our invoices will of course have to be in whole pounds and pennies. So that our software is correctly designed, could you remind me of the rules on rounding amounts of VAT?

Tasks

(a)   Complete Iris Ltd's VAT return for the period.
(b)   Reply to the Senior Accountant's memorandum.
(c)   Reply to the finance director's memorandum.
(d)   Reply to the second memorandum from the data processing manager.

A blank VAT return is provided below.

Value Added Tax Return

For the period
01 10 X5 to 31 12 X5

For Official Use

Registration number	Period
653 5306 77	12 X5

You could be liable to a financial penalty if your completed return and all the VAT payable are not received by the due date.

Due date: 31 01 X6

For Official Use	

IRIS LTD
1 FLOWER STREET
BLOOMTOWN
BL1 4LN

Your VAT Office telephone number is 0123-4567

Before you fill in this form please read the notes on the back and the VAT Leaflet *"Filling in your VAT return"*.
Fill in all boxes clearly in ink, and write 'none' where necessary. Don't put a dash or leave any box blank. If there are no pence write "00" in the pence column. Do not enter more than one amount in any box.

			£	p
For official use	VAT due in this period on sales and other outputs	1		
	VAT due in this period on acquisitions from other EC Member States	2		
	Total VAT due (the sum of boxes 1 and 2)	3		
	VAT reclaimed in this period on purchases and other inputs (including acquisitions from the EC)	4		
	Net VAT to be paid to Customs or reclaimed by you (Difference between boxes 3 and 4)	5		
	Total value of sales and all other outputs excluding any VAT. Include your box 8 figure	6		00
	Total value of purchases and all other inputs excluding any VAT. Include your box 9 figure	7		00
	Total value of all supplies of goods and related services, excluding any VAT, to other EC Member States	8		00
	Total value of all acquisitions of goods and related services, excluding any VAT, from other EC Member States	9		00

Retail schemes. If you have used any of the schemes in the period covered by this return, enter the relevant letter(s) in this box.

If you are enclosing a payment please tick this box.	DECLARATION: You, or someone on your behalf, must sign below.
	I, ... declare that the
	(Full name of signatory in BLOCK LETTERS)
	information given above is true and complete.
	Signature.. Date 20
	A false declaration can result in prosecution.

Trial Run Devolved Assessment 1:Myllton Ltd (data and tasks)

Performance criteria

The following performance criteria are covered in this Trial Run Devolved Assessment.

Element 7.1: Prepare and present periodic performance reports

1   Information derived from different units of the organisation is consolidated into the appropriate form.

2   Information derived from different information systems within the organisation is correctly reconciled.

3   When comparing results over time an appropriate method which allows for changing price levels is used.

4   Transactions between separate units of the organisation are accounted for in accordance with the organisation's procedures.

5   Ratios and performance indicators are accurately calculated in accordance with the organisation's procedures.

6   Reports are prepared in the appropriate form and presented to management within required timescales.

Element 7.2: Prepare reports and returns for outside agencies

1   Relevant information is identified, collated and presented in accordance with the conventions and definitions used by outside agencies.

2   Calculations of ratios and performance indicators are accurate.

3   Authorisation for the despatch of completed reports and returns is sought from the appropriate person.

4   Reports and returns are presented in accordance with outside agencies' requirements and deadlines.

Element 7.3: Prepare VAT returns

1   VAT returns are correctly completed using data from the appropriate recording systems and are submitted within the statutory time limits.

2   Relevant inputs and outputs are correctly identified and calculated.

3   Submissions are made in accordance with current legislation.

4   Guidance is sought from the VAT office when required, in a professional manner.

Trial Run Devolved Assessment
1 Myllton Ltd

Instructions

This Assessment is designed to test your ability to prepare reports and returns.

The situation is provided on page 46.

The tasks to be completed are set out on pages 47 to 50.

The Assessment contains a large volume of data which you will require in order to complete the tasks.

Your answers should be set out in the answer booklet, on pages 53 to 60, using the answer sheets provided.

You are allowed **three hours** to complete your work.

A high level of accuracy is required.

Correcting fluid may be used, but it should be used in moderation. Errors should be crossed out neatly and clearly. You should write in black ink, not pencil.

The information you require is provided as far as possible in the sequence in which you will need to deal with it. However, you are advised to look quickly through all of the material before you begin. This will help you to familiarise yourself with the situation and the information available.

You are reminded that you should not use any unauthorised material, such as books or notes, during this Assessment.

A full answer to this Assessment is provided on page 139. Do not turn to the suggested answer until you have completed all parts of the Assessment.

BPP PUBLISHING

THE SITUATION

Your name is Olivia Tran and you work as the Deputy Accountant at Myllton Ltd, 23 Cavour Road, Bridge Trading Estate, New Sarum SPO 7YT.

Myllton Ltd manufactures timber window and door frames which are sold to the building trade.

Myllton Ltd is an autonomous subsidiary company within the Hexa-Gann Group Plc.

Your immediate superior is James Mbanu, the Company Accountant. James reports to Romy Gurlane, Myllton Ltd's Managing Director.

Myllton Ltd is separately registered for VAT; there is no group registration in force. All sales, which are all to UK customers, are standard-rated. The company's local VAT office is at Roebuck House, 24-28 Bedford Place, Southampton SO15 2DB.

A small part of Myllton Ltd's sales are to Jevonille Ltd, a large builders merchants, which is also part of the Hexa-Gann Group. All the timber used by Myllton Ltd is supplied by Graviner Ltd, another group company.

Myllton Ltd has an efficient production control system and a rapid flow of products through the factory. It is, therefore, unnecessary to carry any significant stocks of materials or finished products.

Production is labour intensive. Myllton operates a standard costing system and output is measured in standard hours.

The financial year end for all Hexa-Gann Group companies is 31 December.

Today's date is Monday 2 August 2000.

Task 1

The transfer price of timber from Graviner Ltd to Myllton Ltd has remained unchanged since 1995.

Romy Gurlane believes that the drop in timber prices since 1995 means that Myllton Ltd has been overcharged by Graviner Ltd. Romy is particularly concerned because the Managing Director's annual bonus is based on the Return on Capital Employed achieved by the company in the financial year.

Set out below are the figures for purchases of timber by Myllton Ltd from Graviner Ltd during 1999, together with the relevant price index taken from the June 2000 edition of the *Monthly Digest of Statistics.*

You are required to use these figures to complete the form on page 53 of the answer booklet.

1999	Invoiced purchases of timber from Graviner Ltd, including VAT £'000	Index of materials purchased by the Wood and Wood Products Industry *1995 =100*
January	138	96.9
February	173	96.2
March	147	95.8
April	171	95.8
May	138	95.7
June	232	95.5
July	209	95.2
August	196	95.0
September	274	94.6
October	225	94.3
November	201	94.4
December	183	94.4
Total	2,287	n/a

Task 2

You are required to calculate the total value of timber purchased by Myllton Ltd from Graviner Ltd during 1999 at 1999 prices, excluding VAT.

Use the figures you have obtained in Task 1.

Use the form provided on page 54 of the answer booklet and calculate the figures to the nearest £'000 at each step.

Task 3

The following information has been extracted from Myllton Ltd's annual accounts for 1999 and passed to you for analysis. All figures exclude VAT.

	£'000
Sales	4,264
Timber purchases from Graviner Ltd	1,946
Other material purchases	328
Production labour	739
Production overheads	254
Administration overheads	476
Selling and distribution costs	198
Other non-production costs	57
Fixed assets (net book value)	1,847
Current assets	638
Current liabilities	204

You are required to write a memo to Romy Gurlane showing the effect that Graviner Ltd's use of 1995 values for transfer prices has had on the following ratios.

- The gross profit percentage for 1999
- The net profit percentage for 1999
- The return on capital employed for 1999

You should present the ratios in two columns

- In column one use the figures contained in the 1999 accounts
- In column two show what the figures would be if the timber purchased from Graviner Ltd was valued at 1999 prices instead of 1995 prices, ie using the figure you calculated in Task 2

Task 4

The Hexa-Gann Group Plc is a member of the Timber and Ancillary Trades Federation (TATF). Myllton Ltd and Graviner Ltd are the only companies within the group whose activities fall within the ambit of the TATF. Consequently, any figures requested by the TATF are provided by combining Myllton Ltd and Graviner Ltd's figures into one return on behalf of the Hexa-Gann Group Plc.

Hexa-Gann Group Plc's membership number is H920/58

Myllton Ltd acts as the reporting point for returns to the TATF.

You are given the following figures, which have been taken from Graviner Ltd's annual accounts for 1999. All these figures are compatible with those for Myllton Ltd contained in Task 3.

	£'000
Sales (including sales to other members of the Hexa-Gann Group)	13,420
Timber purchases (all from outside the Hexa-Gann Group)	7,938
Other material purchases	276
Production labour	1,260
Production overheads	319
Administration overheads	684
Selling and distribution costs	276
Other non-production costs	147

On page 56 in the answer booklet you will find a form sent to Hexa-Gann Group Plc by the TATF. You are required to complete this form by combining the figures for Myllton Ltd provided in Task 3 with those for Graviner Ltd above. You should exclude any inter-group purchases or sales between Myllton Ltd and Graviner Ltd, to avoid double counting. Myllton made no sales to Graviner during 1999.

Task 5

Use the memo form on page 57 of the answer booklet to pass the TATF form that you completed in Task 4 to Nigel Lyte (who is the Company Secretary for the Hexa-Gann Group Plc) seeking his signature and authorisation for its despatch by Special Delivery. You should point out that the due date for the return is near.

Task 6

Set out below are figures relating to production and hours worked in the previous three months. You are required to use these figures to complete the table on page 58 of the answer booklet.

Month 2000	Standard hours produced	Production labour hours worked
March	7,236	7,539
April	6,208	6,514
May	6,836	7,258
June	6,871	6,943
July	7,633	7,429

Task 7

You are required to complete the VAT return on page 59 of the answer booklet for Myllton Ltd in respect of the quarter ended 31 July 2000. You have obtained the following information.

Period - 1 May 2000 to 31 July 2000	Excluding VAT	VAT
	£	£
Sales, all to UK customers	1,066,327.67	186,607.34
Purchases from UK suppliers	703,156.21	105,473.43
Purchase of car included above	28,450.90	4,978.90
Acquisitions from other EC member states	13,094.50	2,291.54
VAT bad debt relief being claimed		738.76

Notes.
1.   All sales were to UK customers
2.   The purchases include some zero rated and exempt supplies
3.   The car was purchased for the use of Romy Gurlane. It will be used for private as well as business purposes
4.   Payment will be included with the return
5.   The return is to be signed by James Mbanu

Task 8

Myllton Ltd has arranged a canal boat trip, to take place on 31 August 2000, for its staff and representatives of its customers. An evening meal will be provided, together with music and a free bar. This is a standard package supplied by Knet Cruises Ltd, who are registered for VAT.

As VAT can only be reclaimed in respect of staff entertainment you are required to draft a letter to your local VAT office seeking advice on the correct treatment of the VAT element of the Knet Cruises invoice.

Use the blank letterhead provided on page 60 of the answer booklet.

Answer booklet for Trial Run Devolved Assessment 1 (Myllton Ltd)

ANSWER BOOKLET FOR TRIAL RUN DEVOLVED ASSESSMENT 1: MYLLTON LTD

Task 1

Calculation of purchases of timber from Graviner Ltd using 1999 prices.

1998	Monthly purchases at invoiced prices, including VAT £'000	Index of materials purchased by the Wood and Wood Products Industry, 1995 =100	Value of timber purchases at current prices, including VAT £'000
January			
February			
March			
April			
May			
June			
July			
August			
September			
October			
November			
December			
Total			

Notes.
1. The first column should contain the monthly invoiced purchases of timber from Graviner Ltd, including VAT, which use transfer prices agreed in 1995.
2. The second column should contain the monthly figures for the Index of prices of materials purchased by the Wood and Wood Products Industry, where 1995 = 100.
3. The third column will contain your calculated value of the invoiced purchases from Graviner Ltd if current prices had been used instead of those set in 1995.
4. Show each monthly purchases figure in column three to the nearest £'000. Your total for column three should be the sum of the monthly figures shown in that column.

Task 2

	£'000
Value of timber purchases at current prices, including VAT	
VAT included above at 17.5%	
Value of timber purchases at current prices, excluding VAT	

Task 3

MEMO

To:

From:

Subject:

Date:

_____

_____

_____

_____

_____

_____

_____

_____

_____

_____

_____

_____

_____

_____

_____

_____

_____

_____

_____

BPP PUBLISHING

Task 4

Timber and Ancillary Trades Federation

Gloster House, 33 Loville Road, Dartford, Kent DA8 3QQ

TURNOVER AND COSTS RETURN 1999

Company or Business Name	
Membership number	
Accounting year end date	
Period covered by figures, if less than one year	
	£m
Turnover	
Timber purchases	
Production labour costs	
Other production costs	
Non-production costs	
Total costs	

Notes.
1. All figures should exclude VAT.
2. All figures should be to the nearest £100,000 and expressed as decimal millions (eg £31,832,420 would be £31.8)
3. This return should be signed by an officer of the company, or the owner or a partner if unincorporated.

Signature:	
Name:	
Position:	
Date:	

Please return to Annabelle Peruke at the above address by 6 August 2000, marked 'Private & Confidential'.

Task 5

MEMO

To:

From:

Subject:

Date:

Task 6

<table>
<tr><td colspan="4" align="center">**MYLLTON LTD**

PRODUCTIVITY REPORT</td></tr>
<tr><td>**Period**</td><td>**Standard hours produced (3 month total)**</td><td>**Production labour hours worked, (3 month total)**</td><td>**Output hours per input hour**</td></tr>
<tr><td>March 00 to May 00</td><td></td><td></td><td></td></tr>
<tr><td>April 00 to June 00</td><td></td><td></td><td></td></tr>
<tr><td>May 00 to July 00</td><td></td><td></td><td></td></tr>
</table>

Note. The productivity ratio is to be expressed to three decimal places.

Task 7

Value Added Tax Return
For the period
01 05 00 to 31 07 00

For Official Use

Registration number | Period
578 4060 20 | 07 00

You could be liable to a financial penalty if your completed return and all the VAT payable are not received by the due date.

081 578 4060 19 100 03 98   Q35192

James Mbanu
Myllton Ltd
23 Cavour Road
Bridge Trading Estate
New Sarum SP0 7YT   219921/10

Due date: 31 08 00

For
Official
Use

Your VAT Office telephone number is 01682-386000

Before you fill in this form please read the notes on the back and the VAT Leaflet *"Filling in your VAT return"*.
Fill in all boxes clearly in ink, and write 'none' where necessary. Don't put a dash or leave any box blank. If there are no pence write "00" in the pence column. Do not enter more than one amount in any box.

			£	p
For official use	VAT due in this period on sales and other outputs	**1**		
	VAT due in this period on acquisitions from other EC Member States	**2**		
	Total VAT due (the sum of boxes 1 and 2)	**3**		
	VAT reclaimed in this period on purchases and other inputs (including acquisitions from the EC)	**4**		
	Net VAT to be paid to Customs or reclaimed by you (Difference between boxes 3 and 4)	**5**		
	Total value of sales and all other outputs excluding any VAT. Include your box 8 figure	**6**		00
	Total value of purchases and all other inputs excluding any VAT. Include your box 9 figure	**7**		00
	Total value of all supplies of goods and related services, excluding any VAT, to other EC Member States	**8**		00
	Total value of all acquisitions of goods and related services, excluding any VAT, from other EC Member States	**9**		00

Retail schemes. If you have used any ot the schemes in the period covered by this return, enter the relevant letter(s) in this box.

If you are enclosing a payment please tick this box.	DECLARATION: You, or someone on your behalf, must sign below.
	I, ... declare that the (Full name of signatory in BLOCK LETTERS) information given above is true and complete. Signature....................................... Date .... 20 **A false declaration can result in prosecution.**

B

0196929   PCU(November 1995)

VAT 100 (Half)

BPP PUBLISHING

Task 8

MYLLTON LTD

23 Cavour Road, Bridge Trading Estate, New Sarum SPO 7YT
Telephone 01722-883567

_____

_____

_____

_____

_____

_____

_____

_____

_____

_____

_____

_____

_____

_____

_____

_____

_____

_____

_____

_____

Registered office: 23 Cavour Road, Bridge Trading Estate, New Sarum SPO 7YT
Registered in England, number 2314562

Trial Run Devolved Assessment 2: Lanbergis Hire Ltd (data and tasks)

Performance criteria

The following performance criteria are covered in this Trial Run Devolved Assessment.

Element 7.1: Prepare and present periodic performance reports

1 Information derived from different units of the organisation is consolidated into the appropriate form.

2 Information derived from different information systems within the organisation is correctly reconciled.

3 When comparing results over time an appropriate method which allows for changing price levels is used.

4 Transactions between separate units of the organisation are accounted for in accordance with the organisation's procedures.

5 Ratios and performance indicators are accurately calculated in accordance with the organisation's procedures.

6 Reports are prepared in the appropriate form and presented to management within required timescales.

Element 7.2: Prepare reports and returns for outside agencies

1 Relevant information is identified, collated and presented in accordance with the conventions and definitions used by outside agencies.

2 Calculations of ratios and performance indicators are accurate.

3 Authorisation for the despatch of completed reports and returns is sought from the appropriate person.

4 Reports and returns are presented in accordance with outside agencies' requirements and deadlines.

Element 7.3: Prepare VAT returns

1 VAT returns are correctly completed using data from the appropriate recording systems and are submitted within the statutory time limits.

2 Relevant inputs and outputs are correctly identified and calculated.

3 Submissions are made in accordance with current legislation.

4 Guidance is sought from the VAT office when required, in a professional manner.

Trial Run Devolved Assessment
2 Lanbergis Hire Ltd

Instructions

This assessment is designed to test your ability to prepare reports and returns.

The situation is provided on page 64.

The tasks to be completed are set out on pages 65 to 70.

The assessment contains a large volume of data which you will require in order to complete the tasks.

Your answers should be set out in the answer booklet, on pages 73 to 79, using the answer sheets provided.

You are allowed **three hours** to complete your work.

A high level of accuracy is required.

Correcting fluid may be used, but it should be used in moderation. Errors should be crossed out neatly and clearly. You should write in black ink, not pencil.

The information you require is provided as far as possible in the sequence in which you will need to deal with it. However, you are advised to look quickly through all of the material before you begin. This will help you to familiarise yourself with the situation and the information available.

You are reminded that you should not use any unauthorised material, such as books or notes during this Trial Run Devolved Assessment.

A full answer to this Assessment is provided on page 147. Do not turn to the suggested answer until you have completed all parts of the Assessment.

BPP PUBLISHING

THE SITUATION

Your name is Eric Kendall. You are employed as a temporary accountant by **Lanbergis Hire Ltd** of 71 Marefair, Lanbergis Outcastle XA32 7DD. You have been engaged to provide holiday cover for Barbara Mandeville, the Accountant, who reports to Raju Shah, the **Managing Director** of Lanbergis Hire Ltd. Barbara is on holiday from 7 to 22 August 2000.

The company rents out cars to business and private customers, on a daily and weekly basis, as well as hiring out cars on long-term leases.

Lanbergis Hire Ltd's customers must pay for all petrol consumed, in addition to the rental or leasing charge.

Lanbergis Hire Ltd, is a wholly owned subsidiary company of Ghent & Cheny Plc.

Lanbergis Hire Ltd shares the 71 Marefair site with another Ghent & Cheny subsidiary, Outcastle Auto Ltd. Outcastle Auto Ltd has several car repair workshops in the district, though its main workshop is at 71 Marefair.

Outcastle Auto Ltd has its own Managing Director, Wendy Clarke, but some administrative functions are carried out by Lanbergis Hire Ltd on Outcastle Auto Ltd's behalf. There is a considerable amount of inter-company trading, with Lanbergis Hire Ltd's cars being repaired by Outcastle Auto and Lanbergis Hire providing courtesy cars for Outcastle Auto Ltd.

Lanbergis Hire Ltd and Outcastle Auto Ltd are registered as a group for VAT purposes. Lanbergis Hire Ltd acts as the representative member of the group. The company's local VAT office is at 2nd Floor, Tower Chambers, 31 Skew Road, Kirkmanor XA3 9TY.

Lanbergis Hire Ltd's VAT registration number is 578 4060 21.

The financial year end for all Ghent & Cheny group companies is 30 June.

Today's date is Monday 16 August 2000.

Task 1

Raju Shah is reviewing Lanbergis Hire Ltd's charges for daily and weekly car hire. The company has not changed its prices since September 1999. Raju has asked you, in Barbara's absence, to investigate the changes in UK motoring costs since September 1999. Raju will then compare this data with Lanbergis Hire's own changes in costs since September 1999.

Raja has asked you to produce separate figures for running costs and for car purchase prices.

Set out below is an extract from Table 18.2, Retail Prices Index, taken from the June 2000 edition of the *Monthly Digest of Statistics.*

	Group and sub-group weights in 2000	1999	1999	1999	1999	2000	2000	2000	2000
		Sep	*Oct*	*Nov*	*Dec*	*Jan*	*Feb*	*Mar*	*Apr*
Motoring expenditure	139	171.5	170.6	169.6	168.0	169.6	169.4	172.4	175.8
Purchase of motor vehicles	58	139.2	137.9	136.6	134.6	137.1	137.0	136.8	137.1
Maintenance of motor vehicles	23	196.8	197.0	197.0	197.4	198.4	198.7	199.6	200.7
Petrol and oil	38	192.7	192.2	190.7	188.0	186.3	185.5	196.1	206.4
Vehicle tax and insurance	20	213.3	211.3	211.3	211.3	217.5	217.5	220.0	224.9

You are required to construct an index of vehicle running costs, excluding depreciation, petrol and oil, by combining the index for the maintenance of motor vehicles with that for vehicle tax and insurance.

Use the weights contained in the above table.

Enter your results in the form on page 73 of the answer booklet.

Task 2

You are required to take the 'Vehicle running costs index' that you created in Task 1 and re-base it, with September 1999 as 100.

Do the same for the 'Purchase of motor vehicles index'.

Enter your indices in the form contained on page 73 of the answer booket.

BPP PUBLISHING

Task 3

You are required to write a short informal report to Raju explaining what you have done and noting your findings.

Refer to the table that you produced in Task 2, which you will submit as an attachment to your report.

Give two reasons why the motoring expenditure index contained in the data for Task 1 would not provide a reliable comparison with the changes in the costs to Lanbergis Hire of operating its fleet of hire cars.

Briefly explain how a single index could be calculated from the components used to construct the motoring expenditure index which would reflect more accurately Lanbergis Hire's cost structure and so provide a better basis for comparison with its own cost changes.

Use the memo form on page 74 of the answer booklet. Continue on a separate sheet if necessary.

Task 4

Kirkmanor District Council levy charges for the collection and disposal of industrial waste. The charge is based on a formula combining the volume and tonnage of waste collected with the business's value added figure. Whilst Kirkmanor District Council has its own data for the weight and volume of waste collected from each location, it needs data on the value added by the businesses at each location to calculate the correct charge. It obtains this information by issuing a questionnaire every half year.

You are given the following data for the six months ended 30 June 2000. All figures exclude VAT.

	Lanbergis Hire Ltd	Outcastle Auto Ltd
	£	£
Turnover	1,427,602	1,398,717
Sales to Outcastle Auto included in turnover	18,376	
Sales to Lanbergis Hire included in turnover		43,524
Disposals of capital goods included in turnover	89,320	1,513
Purchases of goods and services, including inter-company transactions	1,042,836	972,374
Purchases of capital goods included in 'purchases of goods and services'	382,718	19,421

You are required to complete the questionnaire on page 75 of the answer booklet in respect of the activities carried out at 71 Marefair.

The value added figure for both businesses should be combined.

Exclude any inter-company trading between Lanbergis Hire and Outcastle Auto.

Task 5

You are required to write a memo to Raju Shah seeking his signature and authority to despatch the value added questionnaire to Kirkmanor District Council.

Alert Raju to the due date for the return of the questionnaire.

BPP
PUBLISHING

Task 6

One set of measures of operating efficiency employed by Lanbergis Hire are the percentage availability and utilisation of its vehicles. These figures are calculated weekly.

Two figures are produced

- Availability, defined as 'car-days' available for hiring or leasing as a percentage of car-days in Lanbergis Hire Ltd's ownership
- Hire days as a percentage of available car-days.

The week runs from Monday to Sunday. Lanbergis Hire Ltd are open seven days a week.

Lanbergis Hire Ltd had 72 cars on its books at the beginning of last week.

During that week one car was written off in an accident on Tuesday evening. Ownership immediately passed to Lanbergis Hire Ltd's insurance company under the terms of their policy.

Another car broke down early on Wednesday morning. It was still being repaired in Outcastle Auto Ltd's workshop at the end of the week.

Lanbergis Hire Ltd took delivery of six new cars early on Tuesday morning, these were given a pre-hire service by Outcastle Auto Ltd during Tuesday and Wednesday and were handed over to clients on long-term leases on Thursday morning.

Four cars were sold on Friday afternoon. They were taken out of service on Thursday morning for pre-sale cleaning and servicing by Outcastle Auto Ltd.

Sixteen cars were on long-term leases at the beginning of the week .

One car was returned on Wednesday evening when its lease expired. It was one of the four cars which were sold on Friday.

During the week there were the following short-term rentals, in addition to the long-term leasings.
- 33 one-day hirings
- 34 two-day hirings
- 15 three-day hirings
- 8 four-day hirings
- 4 five-day hirings
- 2 six-day hirings
- 17 seven-day hirings

You are required to complete last week's vehicle utilisation report.

Use the form on page 77 of the answer booklet.

Task 7

Ghent & Cheny Plc has an American subsidiary company, San Luis Exchange Inc. Cary Levinson, one of San Luis Exchange Inc.'s overseas sales staff is about to conduct a protracted business tour of Scandinavia and Northern Europe, including the UK, where he also plans to take a holiday.

Lanbergis Hire Ltd has a car belonging to Harller AB, a Swedish member of the Ghent & Cheny Group which is also a car hire business. The car was left in England by a customer of Harller AB on 7 August 2000. It would normally cost approximately £800 to have the car returned to Sweden.

As Cary is visiting Lanbergis Hire Ltd on 18 August it has been agreed that he can return the car to Harller AB. Cary is particularly keen on the arrangement as he dislikes right-hand drive cars. However, in the absence of the Harller AB car, company policy would dictate that Cary would have to hire a car from Lanbergis Hire Ltd.

Cary will take possession of the car on 18 August as he intends to use it during a holiday in Scotland. He will then use the car while visiting clients in Britain, Denmark, Norway and Sweden, before handing it back to Harller AB. Cary estimates that this arrangement will save San Luis Exchange Inc. about £600 and himself about £400 in car rental fees.

The accounting for this car rental/delivery activity appears complex. Raju Shah has suggested two alternative charging options to recover the loss of the car rental which San Luis Exchange and Cary would otherwise have paid.

- Lanbergis Hire Ltd to charge San Luis Exchange Inc. £1,000, and San Luis Exchange Inc. to charge Harller AB £800
- Lanbergis Hire Ltd to charge Harller AB £800 and San Luis Exchange Inc. £200.

It would be left to San Luis Exchange Inc., in either case, to recover the value of the private use from Cary if the company wished.

You are required to write to the local VAT office explaining the situation and seeking their advice as to how each option should be treated for VAT.

Use the blank letterhead provided on page 78 of the answer booklet. Use a continuation sheet if necessary.

Task 8

Barbara Mandeville extracted the following figures from Lanbergis Hire Ltd's and Outcastle Auto Ltd's accounting records as she intended to complete the VAT return before she went on holiday.

In the event, the job was not done and it has been left to you to prepare the VAT return for Barbara's signature when she gets back.

All figures relate to the period 1 May 2000 to 31 July 2000.

There were no purchases from, or sales to, EC or overseas suppliers or customers.

A cheque for any VAT due will accompany the completed return.

	Lanbergis Hire Ltd £	Outcastle Auto Ltd £
Turnover, excluding VAT	815,928.42	699,358.57
Sales to Outcastle Auto included in turnover	12,736.00	
Sales to Lanbergis Hire included in turnover		28,452.75
Disposals of cars, including VAT, not included in turnover	38,187.50	
Purchases, including inter-company transactions, excluding VAT	494,814.67	476,781.92
VAT on purchases	74,212.70	71,517.15
Cars purchased, excluding VAT, not included in 'purchases'	189,723.00	
VAT on cars purchased.	33,201.52	

Notes.
1. All supplies by both companies were subject to VAT at the standard rate.
2. All cars were purchased for use as hire cars or for leasing to customers.

You are required to complete the VAT return on page 79 of the answer booklet.

Answer booklet for Trial Run Devolved Assessment 2 (Lanbergis Hire Ltd)

ANSWER BOOKLET FOR TRIAL RUN DEVOLVED ASSESSMENT 2: LANBERGIS HIRE LTD

Task 1

Vehicle running costs index, 13 January 1988 = 100

Year	1999	1999	1999	1999	2000	2000	2000	2000
Month	Sep	Oct	Nov	Dec	Jan	Feb	Mar	Apr
Vehicle running costs index								

Task 2

Purchase of motor vehicles index and Vehicle running costs index
Re-based to September 1999 =100

Year	1999	1999	1999	1999	2000	2000	2000	2000
Month	Sep	Oct	Nov	Dec	Jan	Feb	Mar	Apr
Purchase of motor vehicles index, Sep 1999 = 100								
Vehicle running costs index, Sep 1999 = 100								

Task 3

MEMO

To:

From:

Subject:

Date:

_____

_____

_____

_____

_____

_____

_____

_____

_____

_____

_____

_____

_____

_____

_____

_____

_____

_____

_____

_____

_____

Task 4

Kirkmanor District Council
Environmental Services Department
Town Hall, Kirkmanor XA3 9RS

Value Added Questionnaire - Strictly Confidential

The following information is required to enable the charge for the collection of industrial and commercial waste to be calculated. Failure to reply within 60 days of the designated period end will result in an estimated charge which may exceed considerably that which would normally be payable.

Where waste from more than one business is collected from the same location it will be necessary to consolidate the figures for all businesses operating from that location.

This questionnaire must be completed twice per calendar year, in respect of the six-month period ending 30 June and again in respect of the six month period ending 31 December. In the case of commencement or cessation of a business the questionnaire should be completed to or from the half-year date closest to the date of commencement or cessation.

Company or Business Name(s)	
Full postal address of location from which waste is collected.	
Period covered by this questionnaire	
Turnover, excluding VAT	£
Value added	£

For the purposes of this questionnaire
- *Turnover* should exclude the proceeds from the disposal of capital goods, land and buildings, and all transactions between businesses operating from the same location.
- *Capital goods* are defined as fixed assets which are eligible for capital allowances in the calculation of income tax or corporation tax.
- *Value added* is defined as Turnover, excluding VAT, less Purchased Inputs excluding VAT.
- *Purchased inputs* should exclude purchases of capital goods, land and buildings and transactions between businesses operating from the same location.

Signature of authorised person	Date
Name	Position

The information contained in this questionnaire is confidential and will not be used for any other purpose.

BPP
PUBLISHING

Task 5

MEMO

To:

From:

Subject:

Date:

_____

_____

_____

_____

_____

_____

_____

_____

_____

_____

_____

_____

_____

_____

_____

_____

_____

_____

Task 6

LANBERGIS HIRE LTD

VEHICLE UTILISATION REPORT

WEEK ENDING Sunday ....

1. Car-days in company ownership	
2. Car-days unavailable due to servicing & repairs	
3. Car-days available for hire or leasing (1 minus 2)	
4. Availability percentage (3 as % of 1)	
5. Car-days on long-term leases	
6. Car-days on short-term rentals	
7. Car-days hired out or leased (5 plus 6)	
8. Hire-days percentage (7 as % of 3)	
Report completed by:	Date:

Notes.
1. The percentages are to be expressed to one decimal place.
2. Do not use fractions of days. Events occurring before midday are treated as occurring at 00.01 hours. Events occurring after midday are treated as occurring at 24.00 hours.

Task 7

Lanbergis Hire Ltd
71 Marefair, Lanbergis Outcastle XA32 7DD
Telephone 01898-883567

Registered office: 71 Marefair, Lanbergis Outcastle XA32 7DD
Registered in England, number 2314563

Task 8

Value Added Tax Return

For the period
01 05 00 to 31 07 00

For Official Use

Registration number

578 4060 21

Period

07 00

You could be liable to a financial penalty if your completed return and all the VAT payable are not received by the due date.

081 578 4060 19 100 03 98   Q35192

Barbara Mandeville
Lanbergis Ltd
71 Marefair
Lanbergis Outcastle
XA32 7DD   219921/10

Due date: 31 08 00

For
Official
Use

Your VAT Office telephone number is 01682-386000

Before you fill in this form please read the notes on the back and the VAT Leaflet *"Filling in your VAT return"*.
Fill in all boxes clearly in ink, and write 'none' where necessary. Don't put a dash or leave any box blank. If there are no pence write "00" in the pence column. Do not enter more than one amount in any box.

For official use			£	p
	VAT due in this period on sales and other outputs	**1**		
	VAT due in this period on acquisitions from other EC Member States	**2**		
	Total VAT due (the sum of boxes 1 and 2)	**3**		
	VAT reclaimed in this period on purchases and other inputs (including acquisitions from the EC)	**4**		
	Net VAT to be paid to Customs or reclaimed by you (Difference between boxes 3 and 4)	**5**		
	Total value of sales and all other outputs excluding any VAT. Include your box 8 figure	**6**		00
	Total value of purchases and all other inputs excluding any VAT. Include your box 9 figure	**7**		00
	Total value of all supplies of goods and related services, excluding any VAT, to other EC Member States	**8**		00
	Total value of all acquisitions of goods and related services, excluding any VAT, from other EC Member States	**9**		00

Retail schemes. If you have used any of the schemes in the period covered by this return, enter the relevant letter(s) in this box.

If you are enclosing a payment please tick this box.

DECLARATION: You, or someone on your behalf, must sign below.
I, ... declare that the
(Full name of signatory in BLOCK LETTERS)
information given above is true and complete.

Signature... Date 20
A false declaration can result in prosecution.

B

0196929   PCU(November 1995)

VAT 100 (Half)

BPP
PUBLISHING

AAT Sample Simulation

Performance criteria

The following performance criteria are covered in this Simulation.

Element 7.1: Prepare and present periodic performance reports

1   Information derived from different units of the organisation is consolidated into the appropriate form.

2   Information derived from different information systems within the organisation is correctly reconciled.

3   When comparing results over time an appropriate method which allows for changing price levels is used.

4   Transactions between separate units of the organisation are accounted for in accordance with the organisation's procedures.

5   Ratios and performance indicators are accurately calculated in accordance with the organisation's procedures.

6   Reports are prepared in the appropriate form and presented to management within required timescales.

Element 7.2: Prepare reports and returns for outside agencies

1   Relevant information is identified, collated and presented in accordance with the conventions and definitions used by outside agencies.

2   Calculations of ratios and performance indicators are accurate.

3   Authorisation for the despatch of completed reports and returns is sought from the appropriate person.

4   Reports and returns are presented in accordance with outside agencies' requirements and deadlines.

Element 7.3: Prepare VAT returns

1   VAT returns are correctly completed using data from the appropriate recording systems and are submitted within the statutory time limits.

2   Relevant inputs and outputs are correctly identified and calculated.

3   Submissions are made in accordance with current legislation.

4   Guidance is sought from the VAT office when required, in a professional manner.

AAT Sample Simulation
Hoddle Ltd

Instructions

This simulation is designed to test your ability to prepare reports and returns.

The simulation contains a large volume of data which you will require in order to complete the tasks. The information you require is provided as far as possible in the sequence in which you will need to deal with it. However, you are advised to look quickly through all of the material before you begin. This will help you to familiarise yourself with the situation and the information available.

Your answers should be set out in the **answer booklet** on pages 95 to 103 using the answer sheets provided.

You are allowed **three hours** to complete your work, although up to 30 minutes extra time may be allowed.

A high level of accuracy is required. Check your work before handing it in.

Correcting fluid may be used but it should be used in moderation. Errors should be crossed out neatly and clearly. You should write in black ink, not pencil.

You are reminded that you should not bring any unauthorised material, such as books or notes, into the simulation. If you have any such material in your possession, you should surrender it to the assessor immediately.

Any instances of misconduct will be brought to the attention the AAT, and discplinary action may be taken.

A full answer to this simulation is provided on page 161.

BPP
PUBLISHING

HODDLE LTD

THE SITUATION

Your name is Sol Bellcamp and you work as an accounts assistant for a printing company, Hoddle Limited. Hoddle Limited is owned 100 per cent by anther printing company, Kelly Limited. You report to the Group Accountant, Sherry Teddingham.

Hoddle Limited manufactures a wide range of printed materials such as cards, brochures and booklets. Most customers are based in the UK, but sales are also made to other countries in the European Union (EU). There are no exports to countries outside the EU. All of the company's purchases come from businesses within the UK.

Hoddle Limited is registered for VAT and it makes both standard-rated and zero-rated supplies to its UK customers. All sales to other EU countries qualify as zero-rated. The company's local VAT office is at Brendon House, 14 Abbey Street, Pexley PY2 3WR.

Kelly Limited is separately registered for VAT; there is no group registration in force. Both companies have an accounting year ending on 31 March. There are no other companies in the Kelly group.

Hoddle Limited is a relatively small company and sometimes suffers from shortage of capacity to complete customers' jobs. In these cases, the printing work is done by Kelly Limited. Kelly then sells the completed product to Hoddle for onward sale to the customer. The sale from Kelly to Hoddle is recorded in the books of each company at cost; Kelly does not charge a profit margin.

In this simulation you are concerned with the accounting year ended 31 March 2000.

- To begin with you will be required to prepare the VAT return for Hoddle Limited in respect of the quarter ended 31 March 2000.

- You will then be required to prepare certain reports, both for internal use and for an external interfirm comparison scheme, covering the whole accounting year ended 31 March 2000. These reports will treat the two companies as a single group; they will contain consolidated figures, not figures for either of the two companies separately.

Today's date is 9 April 2000.

Space for your answers is provided on pages 95 to 103.

Tasks

1   Refer to the documents on pages 86 and 87, which have been received from Hoddle Ltd's suppliers during March 2000. No entries have net been made in Hoddle Ltd's books of account in respect of these documents. You are required to explain how you will treat each one of these documents when preparing Hoddle Ltd's VAT return for the period January to March 2000. Use page 95 for your answer.

2   Refer to the sales day book summary, purchases day book summary, cash book summary and petty cash book summary on page 88. These have been printed out from Hoddle Ltd's computerised accounting system for the period January to March 2000. (You are reminded that these summaries do not include the documents dealt with in task 1.) Refer also to the memo on page 89. Using this information you are required to complete the VAT return of Hoddle Ltd for the quarter ended 31 March 2000. A blank VAT return is provided on page 96.

3   The Group Accountant is considering adoption of the cash accounting scheme for VAT. He believes that Hoddle Limited (though not Kelly Limited) might qualify for the scheme. He has asked you to draft a letter to the VAT office, in his name, requesting certain details of the scheme. He is interested in the turnover limit for the scheme, particularly since Hoddle is a member of a group of companies, and in the effect of the scheme in dealing with bad debts. You are required to draft this letter using the blank letterhead on page 97.

4   Refer to the profit and loss account of Kelly Limited on page 90, which covers the period 1 January to 31 March 2000. You are required to prepare a profit and loss account for the same period in which the results of Hoddle and Kelly are consolidated. Enter your answer on the form provided on page 98 as follows:

* Enter the results of Kelly in the first column of the form.

* Using the information already provided for earlier tasks construct the results of Hoddle Ltd and enter them in the second column. Note that Hoddle Ltd's stock at 1 January 2000 was valued at £14,638, while stock at 31 March 2000 was valued at £16,052.

* Make appropriate adjustments in the third column to eliminate the effects of trading between Kelly and Hoddle.

* Calculate the consolidated figures and enter them in the fourth column.

5   Refer to the information on pages 91 and 92. Using this, and information already provided for earlier tasks, you are required to prepare a report for the accountant on the group results for the year ended 31 March 2000. Your report should contain the following:

* Key ratios: gross profit margin; net profit margin; return on shareholders' capital employed.

* Sales revenue for each quarter, both in actual terms and indexed to a common base.

* A pie chart showing the proportion of annual (unindexed) sales earned in each quarter.

Use page 99 to set out your answer. **Note that you are not required to comment on the results for the year, merely to present them according to the instructions above.**

6   You are required to complete the interfirm comparison form on page 100.

7   You are required to prepare a memo to the group accountant enclosing the interfirm comparison form for authorisation before despatch. Use page 102.

BPP
PUBLISHING

Engineering Supplies Limited

Haddlefield Road, Blaysley CG6 6AW
Tel/fax: 01376 44531

Hoddle Limited
22 Formquard Street
Pexley
PY6 32W

SALES INVOICE NO: *2155*

Date: *27 March 2000*

	£
VAT omitted in error from invoice no 2139	
£2,667.30 @ 17.5%	466.77
Total due	466.77

Terms: net 30 days

VAT registration: 318 1827 58

Alpha Stationery

Ainsdale Centre, Mexton EV1 4DF
Telephone 01392 43215

26 March 2000

1 box transparent folders: red

Total including VAT @ 17.5%	14.84
Amount tendered	20.00
Change	5.16

VAT registration 356 7612 33

JAMIESON & CO

Jamieson House, Baines Road, Gresham GM7 2PQ
Telephone: 01677 35567   Fax: 01677 57640

PROFORMA SALES INVOICE

VAT registration: *412 7553 67*

Hoddle Limited
22 Formguard Street
Pexley
PY6 3QW

For professional services in connection with debt collection

	£
Our fees	350.00
VAT	61.25
Total due	411.25

A VAT invoice will be submitted when the total due is paid in full

HODDLE LIMITED
SALES DAY BOOK SUMMARY
JANUARY TO MARCH 2000

	January £	February £	March £	Total £
UK: Zero-rated	20,091.12	22,397.00	23,018.55	65,506.67
UK: Standard-rated	15,682.30	12,914.03	15,632.98	44,229.31
Other EU	874.12	4,992.66	5,003.82	10,870.60
VAT	2,744.40	2,259.95	2,735.77	7,740.12
Total	39,391.94	42,563.64	46,391.12	128,346.70

HODDLE LIMITED
PURCHASES DAY BOOK SUMMARY
JANUARY TO MARCH 2000

	January £	February £	March £	Total £
Purchases	14,532.11	20,914.33	15,461.77	*50,908.21
Distribution expenses	4,229.04	3,761.20	5,221.43	13,211.67
Administration expenses	5,123.08	2,871.45	3,681.62	11,676.15
Other expenses	1,231.00	1,154.99	997.65	3,383.64
VAT	4,027.97	4,543.22	4,119.34	12,690.53
Total	29,143.20	33,245.19	29,481.81	91,870.20

*This figure includes £18,271 of purchases from Kelly Ltd.

HODDLE LIMITED
CASH BOOK SUMMARY
JANUARY TO MARCH 2000

	January £	February £	March £	Total £
Payments				
To creditors	12,901.37	15,312.70	18,712.44	46,926.51
To petty cash	601.40	555.08	623.81	1,780.29
Wages/salaries	5,882.18	6,017.98	6,114.31	18,014.47
Total	19,384.95	21,885.76	25,450.56	66,721.27
Receipts				
VAT from Customs & Excise	2,998.01			2,998.01
From customers	29,312.44	34,216.08	36,108.77	99,637.29
Total	32,310.45	34,216.08	36,108.77	102,635.30
Surplus for month	12,925.50	12,330.32	10,658.21	
Balance b/f	−8,712.41	4,213.09	16,543.41	
Balance c/f	4,213.09	16,543.41	27,201.62	

HODDLE LIMITED
PETTY CASH BOOK SUMMARY
JANUARY TO MARCH 2000

	January £	February £	March £	Total £
Payments				
Stationery	213.85	80.12	237.58	531.55
Travel	87.34	76.50	102.70	266.54
Office expenses	213.66	324.08	199.51	737.25
VAT	86.55	74.38	84.02	244.95
Total	601.40	555.08	623.81	1,780.29
Receipts from cash book	601.40	555.08	623.81	1,780.29
Surplus for month	0.00	0.00	0.00	
Balance b/f	200.00	200.00	200.00	
Balance c/f	200.00	200.00	200.00	

MEMO

To: Sol Bellcamp

From: Sherry Teddingham

Date: 6 April 2000

Subject: Bad debt - Batty Limited

As you probably know, we have had great difficulty in persuading the above customer to pay what he owes us. We invoiced him in July 1999 for £420 plus VAT at the standard rate, but he has always disputed the debt and it looks as though we will never recover it. We wrote it off to the bad debt account in March of this year, so you should take this into account when preparing the VAT return for the quarter just ended.

KELLY LIMITED
PROFIT AND LOSS ACCOUNT
FOR THE THREE MONTHS ENDED 31 MARCH 2000

	£	£
Sales to external customers		275,601
Sales to Hoddle Limited at cost		*20,167
Total sales		295,768
Opening stock	28,341	
Purchases	136,095	
	164,436	
Closing stock	31,207	
Cost of sales		133,229
Gross profit		162,539
Wages and salaries	47,918	
Distribution expenses	28,341	
Administration expenses	30,189	
Stationery	2,541	
Travel	2,001	
Office expenses	3,908	
Interest payable	12,017	
Other expenses	11,765	
		138,680
Net profit for the period		23,859

*This figure includes £1,896 in respect of a job completed on 31 March 2000 but not delivered to Hoddle Limited until 1 April 2000. It is not included in Hoddle Ltd's purchases for the period ended 31 March.

KELLY AND HODDLE
CONSOLIDATED BALANCE SHEET AT 31 MARCH 2000

	£	£
Fixed assets at net book value		1,229,348
Current assets		
Stock	49,155	
Trade debtors	223,009	
VAT recoverable	13,451	
Cash at bank and in hand	40,088	
	325,703	
Current liabilities		
Trade creditors	136,531	
Other creditors	11,740	
	148,271	
Net current assets		177,432
Total assets less current liabilities		1,406,780
Long term liability		
Loan repayable in 2005		372,072
		1,034,708
Capital and reserves		
Called up share capital		234,167
Retained profits		800,541
		1,034,708

KELLY AND HODDLE
QUARTERLY CONSOLIDATED PROFIT AND LOSS ACCOUNTS
FOR THE YEAR ENDED 31 MARCH 2000

	1 April 1999-30 June 1999 £	1 July 1999-30 September 1999 £	1 October 1999-31 December 1999 £	1 January 2000-31 March 2000 £	1 April 2000-31 March 2000 £
Sales	325,719	275,230	306,321		
Cost of sales	134,861	109,421	121,358		
Gross profit	190,858	165,809	184,963		
Wages and salaries	63,314	61,167	64,412		
Distribution expenses	34,217	30,135	31,221		
Administration expenses	34,765	33,012	36,415		
Stationery	2,981	2,671	3,008		
Travel	1,975	1,876	2,413		
Office expenses	4,412	4,713	3,083		
Interest payable	12,913	12,714	12,432		
Other expenses	10,981	16,421	15,431		
	165,558	162,709	168,415		
Net profit for the period	25,300	3,100	16,548		

Note for candidates: you are advised to complete the above schedule by filling in the figures for the final quarter in the fourth column and totalling the figures to the year in the final column.

MEMO

To: Sol Bellcamp

From: Sherry Teddingham

Subject: Adjusting for the effects of price rises

Date: 2 April 2000

When presenting your quarterly reports on group results please include an item of information additional to that which you normally present. As well as noting sales revenue by quarter, please present quarterly sales revenue adjusted to take account of price rises.

I have identified a suitable index as follows.

First quarter 1998/99 (base period)	231.8
First quarter 1999/00	239.3
Second quarter 1999/00	241.5
Third quarter 1999/00	244.0
Fourth quarter 1999/00	241.8

I will keep you informed of future movements in this index.

Answer booklet for AAT Sample Simulation

ANSWER BOOKLET FOR AAT SIMULATION: HODDLE LTD

Task 1

....

....

....

....

....

....

....

....

....

....

....

....

....

....

....

....

....

....

....

....

....

....

Task 2

Value Added Tax Return

For the period
01 01 00 to 31 03 00

For Official Use

Registration number

578 4060 19

Period

03 00

You could be liable to a financial penalty if your completed return and all the VAT payable are not received by the due date.

081 578 4060 19 100 03 98   Q35192

MR SHERRY TEDDINGHAM
HODDLE LIMITED
22 FORMGUARD STREET
PEXLEY
PY6 3QW   219921/10

Due date: 30 04 00

For
Official
Use

Your VAT Office telephone number is 01682-386000

Before you fill in this form please read the notes on the back and the VAT Leaflet *"Filling in your VAT return"*. Fill in all boxes clearly in ink, and write 'none' where necessary. Don't put a dash or leave any box blank. If there are no pence write "00" in the pence column. Do not enter more than one amount in any box.

For official use		£	p
VAT due in this period on sales and other outputs	**1**		
VAT due in this period on acquisitions from other EC Member States	**2**		
Total VAT due (the sum of boxes 1 and 2)	**3**		
VAT reclaimed in this period on purchases and other inputs (including acquisitions from the EC)	**4**		
Net VAT to be paid to Customs or reclaimed by you (Difference between boxes 3 and 4)	**5**		
Total value of sales and all other outputs excluding any VAT. Include your box 8 figure	**6**		00
Total value of purchases and all other inputs excluding any VAT. Include your box 9 figure	**7**		00
Total value of all supplies of goods and related services, excluding any VAT, to other EC Member States	**8**		00
Total value of all acquisitions of goods and related services, excluding any VAT, from other EC Member States	**9**		00

Retail schemes. If you have used any of the schemes in the period covered by this return, enter the relevant letter(s) in this box.

If you are enclosing a payment please tick this box.

DECLARATION: You, or someone on your behalf, must sign below.

I,... declare that the
(Full name of signatory in BLOCK LETTERS)
information given above is true and complete.

Signature.. Date 20

A false declaration can result in prosecution.

B

0196929   PCU(November 1995)

VAT 100 (Half)

Task 3

HODDLE LIMITED

22 Formguard Street, Pexley PY6 3QW
Telephone 01682 431 432256

....
....
....
....
....
....
....
....
....
....
....
....
....
....
....
....
....
....
....

Registered office: 22 Formguard Street, Pexley PY6 3QW
Registered in England, number 2314561

Task 4

CONSOLIDATED PROFIT AND LOSS ACCOUNT
FOR THE THREE MONTHS ENDED 31 MARCH 2000

	Kelly £	*Hoddle* £	*Adjustments* £	*Consolidated* £
Sales				
Opening stock				
Purchases				
Closing stock				
Cost of sales				
Gross profit				
Wages and salaries				
Distribution expenses				
Administration expenses				
Stationery				
Travel				
Office expenses				
Interest payable				
Other expenses				
Net profit for the period				

Task 5

Task 6

INTERFIRM COMPARISON (IFC) DATA (extracts)

Name of company...

Year ended...

Data

	£	% of sales	Industry best	Industry average
Sales				
Gross profit			62.1%	57.3%
Net profit			10.4%	5.8%
Fixed assets				
Current assets				
Current liabilities				
Return on capital employed			10.3%	9.0%

Important note

Before completing this form you should read the explanatory notes on page 99.

Task 6

COMPLETING THE IFC DATA FORM

Explanatory notes

Note 1

'Sales means sales to external customers. Inter-company, inter-divisional or inter-branch sales should be excluded.

Note 2

Fixed assets should be stated at net book value.

Note 3

Return on capital employed is net profit before interest charges, divided by the total of fixed assets (stated at net book value) and net current assets.

BPP
PUBLISHING

Task 7

....

....

....

....

....

....

....

....

....

....

....

....

....

....

....

....

....

....

....

....

....

....

....

....

Workings sheet

....

....

....

....

....

....

....

....

....

....

....

....

....

....

....

....

....

....

....

....

....

....

....

....

....

Answers to practice activities

Answer to Practice activity 1

COMMA LIMITED
INCOME STATEMENT

| | September 20X2 | | | | 9 months to September 20X2 | | | |
| | Budget | | Actual | | Budget | | Actual | |
	£m	%	£m	%	£m	%	£m	%
Net sales	2.14	100	2.02	100	22.8	100	23.8	100
Less:								
Standard cost	1.12	52	1.02	50	11.6	51	12.3	52
Variances	0.17	8	0.24	12	1.9	8	2.3	10
Other costs	0.19	9	0.23	11	2.7	12	1.9	8
Inter-company contrib	(0.12)	(6)	(0.18)	(9)	(1.6)	(7)	(1.3)	(5)
Manufacturing margin	0.78	36	0.71	35	8.2	36	8.6	36
Selling expenses	0.21	10	0.18	9	2.5	11	2.6	11
Administrative expenses	0.31	14	0.32	16	3.4	15	3.3	14
Inter-company contrib	(0.04)	(2)	(0.02)	(1)	(0.5)	(2)	(0.2)	(1)
Operating income	0.30	14	0.23	11	2.8	12	2.9	12
Inter-company (net)	(0.02)	(1)	0.02	1	(0.2)	(1)	-	-
Income before tax	0.28	13	0.25	12	2.6	11	2.9	12
Tax	0.15	7	0.10	5	1.4	6	1.4	6
Net income	0.13	6	0.15	7	1.2	5	1.5	6

	Last year		Last year	
Net sales	1.85	100	22.4	100
Manufacturing margin	0.61	33	7.8	35
Operating income	0.21	11	2.2	10

Answer to Practice activity 2

Net sales by geographical market 20W6 and 20X1

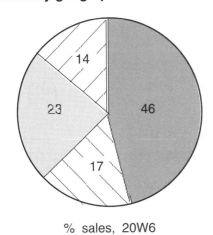

% sales, 20W6   % sales, 20X1

 UK Sales

 EU exports

 North America

 Other

BPP PUBLISHING

Practice activities

Workings

	£'000	*220X1* £'000	%	£'000	*20W6* £'000	%
Home sales		12,249	40		9,273	46
Eire	2,015			-		
Germany	3,605			1,457		
France	2,309			1,200		
Other EU	2,419			894		
EU exports total		10,348	34		3,551	17
Canada	1,722			1,888		
USA	3,402			2,841		
North America		5,124	17		4,729	23
Nigeria	1,521			1,722		
Other non-EU	1,182			1,142		
Other total		2,703	9		2,864	14
		30,424	100		20,417	100

Answer to Practice activity 3

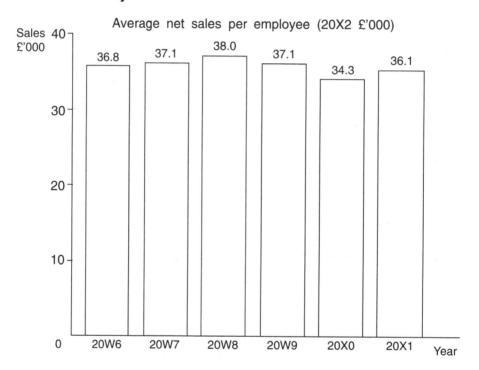

Workings

Total net sales

	£'000			*Current value 20X2* £'000	*Average e'ees*	*Sales per e'ee* £'000
20W6	20,418	× 164.9/128.2	=	26,263	713	36.8
20W7	22,084	× 164.9/132.7	=	27,443	739.5	37.1
20W8	23,783	× 164.9/139.5	=	28,113	764	36.8
20W9	25,621	× 164.9/146.2	=	28,898	789	36.6
20X0	28,088	× 164.9/150.7	=	30,735	896.5	34.3
20X1	30,424	× 164.9/157.8	=	31,793	880.5	36.1

Answer to Practice activity 4

EMERALD TAXIS LTD
SIX MONTHS ENDED 30 JUNE 20X7

KEY FINANCIAL RATIOS

Vehicle	1 SC84 £	2 SC101 £	3 SC105 £	4 SC126 £	5 SC191 £	6 SC213 £	7 SC220 £	8 SC225 £	Overall £
(a) Income per operating mile	0.90	0.91	0.88	0.92	0.85	0.90	0.91	0.91	0.90
(b) Income per operating hour	8.85	9.53	8.98	9.76	7.56	8.51	9.51	9.70	9.09
(c) Income per operating day	80.11	90.49	76.43	88.95	64.28	76.63	85.56	87.85	81.57
(d) Contribution per operating mile	0.41	0.43	0.40	0.46	0.30	0.39	0.45	0.45	0.42
(e) Contribution per operating hour	4.06	4.55	4.06	4.87	2.65	3.73	4.67	4.80	4.21
(f) Contribution per operating day	36.74	43.21	34.58	44.40	22.53	33.61	42.07	43.47	37.82
(g) Variable cost per operating mile	0.49	0.48	0.48	0.46	0.55	0.51	0.46	0.46	0.48
(h) Variable cost per operating hour	4.79	4.98	4.92	4.89	4.91	4.78	4.83	4.90	4.87
(i) Variable cost per operating day	43.37	47.28	41.86	44.55	41.75	43.02	43.48	44.38	43.75
(j) Fixed cost per operating mile	0.26	0.23	0.25	0.23	0.32	0.25	0.24	0.22	0.25
(k) Fixed cost per operating hour	2.59	2.42	2.60	2.43	2.84	2.37	2.51	2.32	2.50
(l) Fixed cost per operating day	23.43	22.97	22.11	22.19	24.16	21.37	22.58	21.05	22.46
(m) Net profit (loss) per operating mile	0.15	0.20	0.14	0.23	(0.02)	0.14	0.21	0.23	0.17
(n) Net profit (loss) per operating hour	1.47	2.13	1.46	2.44	(0.19)	1.36	2.17	2.47	1.71
(o) Net profit (loss) per operating day	13.31	20.24	12.46	22.21	(1.63)	12.24	19.49	22.42	15.36
(p) Percentage net profit to income	16.6%	22.4%	16.3%	25.0%	(2.5%)	16.0%	22.8%	25.5%	18.8%

Answer to Practice activity 5

The total turnover for the period of £115,260 can be analysed into variable costs, fixed costs and net profit as shown below.

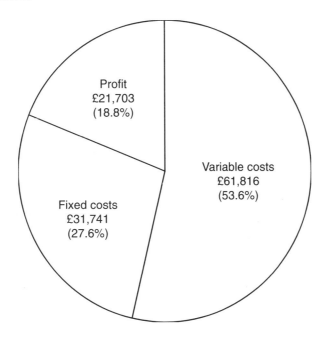

Workings

Vehicle	1	2	3	4	5	6	7	8	Total
	£	£	£	£	£	£	£	£	£
Income	14,500	16,289	13,376	16,100	10,285	13,410	15,400	15,900	115,260
Variable costs									
Fuel	1,210	1,561	1,220	1,310	875	1,077	1,185	1,310	9,748
Wages	6,500	6,800	5,960	6,600	5,440	6,300	6,480	6,560	50,640
Tyres	80	85	75	85	65	81	87	90	648
Maintenance	60	65	70	68	300	70	75	72	780
Total variable costs	7,850	8,511	7,325	8,063	6,680	7,528	7,827	8,032	61,816
Contribution	6,650	7,778	6,051	8,037	3,605	5,882	7,573	7,868	53,444
Fixed costs									
Licence	75	75	75	75	75	75	75	75	600
Reg fee	65	65	65	65	65	65	65	65	520
Insurance	610	700	590	620	575	550	610	560	4,815
Depreciation	1,250	1,050	900	1,000	875	800	1,050	850	7,775
Administration	2,180	2,180	2,180	2,180	2,180	2,180	2,180	2,180	17,440
Maintenance	60	64	60	77	95	70	85	80	591
Total fixed costs	4,240	4,134	3,870	4,017	3,865	3,740	4,065	3,810	31,741
Net profit/(loss)	2,410	3,644	2,181	4,020	(260)	2,142	3,508	4,058	21,703

Pie chart workings

	£	%
Variable costs	61,816	53.6
Fixed costs	31,741	27.6
Profit	21,703	18.8
Turnover	115,260	100.0

Tutorial note. Alternatively, a bar chart could be presented.

Answer to Practice activity 6

VEHICLES RANKED BY NET PROFIT/(LOSS) PER OPERATING DAY

Vehicle	£
SC225	22.42
SC126	22.21
SC101	20.24
SC220	19.49
SC84	13.31
SC105	12.46
SC213	12.24
SC191	(1.63)

Answer to Practice activity 7

Average income per operating mile = £0.90

Average variable costs per operating mile = £0.48

Average fixed cost per vehicle £31,741 ÷ 8 × 2 = £7,935 per annum.

Projected mileage = 36,500
NEW VEHICLE: ESTIMATED ANNUAL INCOME AND COSTS

	£
Income (36,500 × £0.90)	32,850
Less variable costs (36,500 × £0.48)	(17,520)
Contribution	15,330
Fixed costs	(7,935)
Net profit/(loss)	7,395

Answer to Practice activity 8

Inflation factors

20X2	155.1/139.2 = 1.114
20X3	155.1/141.9 = 1.093
20X4	155.1/146.0 = 1.062
20X5	155.1/150.7 = 1.029
20X6	= 1.000

Turnover

	Actual terms	*Real (1996) terms*	*Real annual growth %*
	£	£	
20X2	153,640	171,155	-
20X3	167,040	182,575	6.7
20X4	185,600	197,107	8.0
20X5	201,000	206,829	4.9
20X6	215,000	215,000	4.0

Answer to Practice activity 9

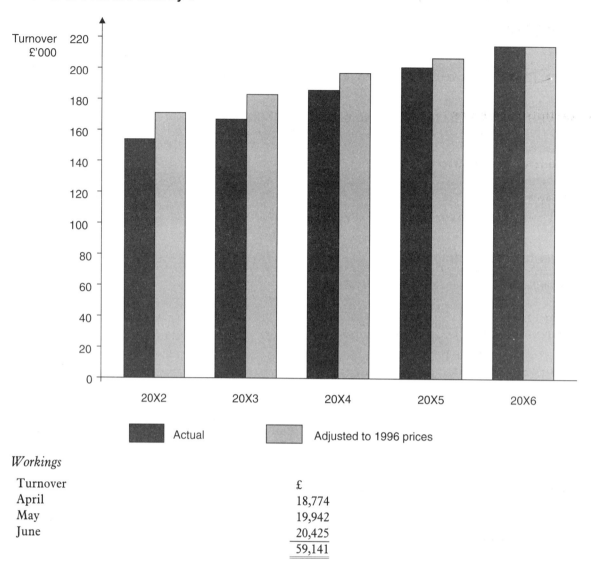

Workings

Turnover	£
April	18,774
May	19,942
June	20,425
	59,141

Answer to Practice Activity 10

NATIONAL TAXI FEDERATION
RETURN FOR SIX MONTHS TO JUNE 20X7
Company name: Emerald Taxis Limited
Membership number: EM002

Performance statistics:	*This period*	*20X6 full year*	*NTF 20X6 average*
Average revenue per vehicle operating day	£81.57	£78.02	£79.70
Average total costs per vehicle operating day	£66.21	£61.07	£60.14
Average revenue per operating mile	£0.90	£0.88	£0.87
Average total costs per operating mile	£0.73	£0.68	£0.67
Net profit as percentage of total revenue	18.8%	17.1%	22.9%
Average mileage per operating day	90.67 miles	88.66 miles	91.84 miles
Average mileage per operating hour	10.10 miles	10.01 miles	9.75 miles

Signed: ....   Date: ....

Please submit this form to NTF Head Office as soon as possible.

Answer to Practice Activity 11

IMPORTANT

Please read the notes before you fill in this form. Give the best estimates you can if you do not have exact figures.

FV			
T15/4 0414000096/941			

1. Details of business

Your business is classified as being in the industry described briefly in the letter accompanying this form. If you think this is wrong, please give a full description of your business. If you are involved in two or more activities, please describe the main one.

2. Period

Period for which you have filled in the form

		Day		Month		Year	
	from	01	/	04	/	X7	11
	to	30	/	06	/	X7	12

3. Turnover to the nearest £thousand (not including VAT)
Total turnover (including fees receivable)

4. Employees

Number of persons employed by the business at the end of the period covered by this return.

4.1	Total employees	10	50

of which

4.2	Full-time male	3	51
4.3	Part-time male	4	52
4.4	Full-time female	3	53
4.5	Part-time female	-	54

5. Other businesses included in this form

The form should be completed for the business named in the covering letter. If, exceptionally, you are unable to limit your return to the activities of this business, please list below the names and VAT registration numbers of the other businesses included.

Name of business   VAT registration number
....
....

(Please continue on a separate sheet if necessary)

REMARKS: If you have given any information which is significantly different from the last quarter, please explain.

PLEASE USE BLOCK CAPITALS
Name of person we should contact if necessary:
Position in business: Date:
Telephone no./ext: Fax/Telex:

Answer to Practice activity 12

RAYTONBANK FOODS LIMITED: HALF YEAR TO JUNE 20X7

Stores	Whitby £	Scarboro £	Stokesley £	Guisboro £	York £	Thirsk £	Malton £	Total £
Ratio								
Turnover per employee	70,382	71,817	71,378	70,844	70,883	70,425	60,000	69,710
Net profit per employee	4,327	4,300	4,222	4,200	4,400	4,175	3,250	4,162
Sales per sq ft	352	345	331	336	315	287	274	322
Wages and salaries per employee	6,200	6,333	6,044	6,022	6,317	6,250	6,250	6,212
Value added	604,000	666,000	484,000	482,000	674,000	440,000	399,000	3,749,000
Value added per employee	10,982	11,100	10,756	10,711	11,233	11,000	9,975	10,867
Value added per £1 of employee costs	1.77	1.75	1.78	1.78	1.78	1.76	1.60	1.75
	%	%	%	%	%	%	%	%
Net profit to sales	6.15	5.99	5.92	5.93	6.21	5.93	5.42	5.97

Answer to Practice activity 13

Productivity measures January - June 20X7 compared with UK grocery retail section

	UK as a whole		Raytonbank
	Year £	$^1/_2$ year £	$^1/_2$ year £
Turnover per employee	140,842	70,421	69,710
Net profit per employee	8,752	4,376	4,162
Wages per full-time employee	13,941	6,971	6,212
Weekly sales per sq ft of sales area	17.00	17.00	12.4

Answer to Practice activity 14

RAYTONBANK FOODS LIMITED
TURNOVER TO EXPENSES AND NET PROFIT
SIX MONTHS TO JUNE 20X7

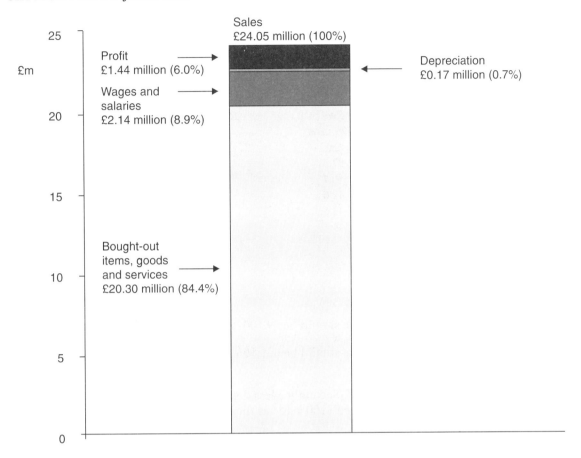

Answer to Practice activity 15

Raytonbank Foods Ltd

Average weekly July sales compared with weekly sales in half year to June 20X7

		Percentage change
(i)	**Sunday opening**	
	Stokesley	+ 13.7
	Guisborough	+ 14.6
	Thirsk	+ 1.9
	Malton	+ 7.6
(ii)	**Non-Sunday opening**	
	Whitby	+ 4.7
	Scarborough	+ 3.0
	York	+ 4.9

Working

	Wh £'000	Sc £'000	St £'000	Gu £'000	Yo £'000	Th £'000	Ma £'000	Total £'000
July sales	625	685	564	565	689	440	396	3,964
Average weekly sales								
Year to June	149	166	124	123	164	108	92	925
July	156	171	141	141	172	110	99	991
Percentage change	+4.7%	+3.0%	+13.7%	+14.6%	+4.9%	+1.9%	+7.6%	+7.1%

Answer to Practice activity 16

Inflation factors

20X2	155.1/139.2	=	1.114
20X3	155.1/141.9	=	1.093
20X4	155.1/146.0	=	1.062
20X5	155.1/150.7	=	1.029
20X6	1.000		

Turnover

	Actual terms £m	*Real (1996) terms* £m	*Real annual growth* %
20X2	33.7	37.5	-
20X3	37.2	40.7	8.5
20X4	40.1	42.6	4.7
20X5	42.3	43.5	2.1
20X6	44.1	44.1	1.4

Answer to Practice activity 17

Errors

Invoice 573:   The amount of VAT due should be £9,100, giving a gross total payable of £61,100.

Invoice 574:   The amount of VAT due should be £21,503.44, giving a gross total payable of £144,380.24.

Invoice from: Silk Ltd   The invoice is not dated. Secondly a less detailed invoice cannot be issued where the goods supplied exceed £100 value as they do in this case.

Answer to Practice activity 18

Output VAT

	£
Invoice to Bar plc	8,504.68
Invoice to Cormick Ltd (corrected amount shown)	9,100.00
Invoice to Work plc (corrected amount shown)	21,503.44
Invoice to Monet plc	40,722.67
	79,830.79
Less credit note to Sole plc	77.00
	79,753.79
Less error in previous period	2,500.00
	77,253.79

Answer to Practice activity 19

Input VAT

	£
Invoice from Tarski plc	29,865.50
Invoice from Course Ltd: £83.60 × 7/47	12.45
Invoice from Silk Ltd: no valid VAT invoice	0.00
Call from public telephone	0.89
Car park fee	2.68
	29,881.52
Less credit note from Tarski plc	210.00
	29,671.52
Bad debt relief on debt from Trib Ltd (over six months old)	665.00
	30,336.52
Less error in previous period	1,600.00
	28,736.52

Answer to Practice activity 20

	£
Invoice to Bar plc	49,590.00
Invoice to Cormick Ltd	52,000.00
Invoice to Work plc	122,876.80
Invoice to Monet plc	237,450.00
	461,916.80
Less credit note to Sole plc	440.00
Total net turnover	461,476.80

Answer to Practice activity 21

	£
Invoice from Tarski plc	170,660.00
Invoice from Course Ltd £83.60 × 40/47	71.15
Invoice from Silk Ltd £270.25 × 40/47	230.00
Expenses	345.97
	171,307.12
Less credit note from Tarski plc	1,200.00
Total net purchases	170,107.12

Answer to Practice activity 22

The net error is £(2,500 − 1,600) = £900, which is not over £2,000 so it may be corrected on the return.

Answer to Practice activity 23

TONK PLC

VAT ACCOUNT FOR THE VAT PERIOD FROM SEPTEMBER TO NOVEMBER 20X7

VAT allowable	£	**VAT payable**	£
Input VAT allowable		Output VAT due	79,830.79
£(29,881.52 - 210.00)	29,671.52	Adjustment for credit	
Correction of error	(1,600.00)	allowed	(77.00)
Refunds for bad debts	665.00	Correction of error	(2,500.00)
	28,736.52		
Cash (payment to HM			77,253.79
Customs & Excise)	48,517.27		
	77,253.79		77,253.79

Answer to Practice activity 24

Value Added Tax Return

For the period
01 09 X7 to 30 11 X7

For Official Use

Registration number: 154 9131 32

Period: 11 X7

You could be liable to a financial penalty if your completed return and all the VAT payable are not received by the due date.

TONK PLC
1 PLINK LANE
INFERTOWN
IN2 4DA

Due date: 31 12 X7

For Official Use

Your VAT Office telephone number is 0123-4567

Before you fill in this form please read the notes on the back and the VAT Leaflet *"Filling in your VAT return".* Fill in all boxes clearly in ink, and write 'none' where necessary. Don't put a dash or leave any box blank. If there are no pence write "00" in the pence column. Do not enter more than one amount in any box.

For official use		£	p
VAT due in this period on sales and other outputs	**1**	77,253	79
VAT due in this period on acquisitions from other EC Member States	**2**	NONE	
Total VAT due (the sum of boxes 1 and 2)	**3**	77,253	79
VAT reclaimed in this period on purchases and other inputs (including acquisitions from the EC)	**4**	28,736	52
Net VAT to be paid to Customs or reclaimed by you (Difference between boxes 3 and 4)	**5**	481,517	27
Total value of sales and all other outputs excluding any VAT. Include your box 8 figure	**6**	461,476	00
Total value of purchases and all other inputs excluding any VAT. Include your box 9 figure	**7**	170,107	00
Total value of all supplies of goods and related services, excluding any VAT, to other EC Member States	**8**	NONE	00
Total value of all acquisitions of goods and related services, excluding any VAT, from other EC Member States	**9**	NONE	00

Retail schemes. If you have used any ot the schemes in the period covered by this return, enter the relevant letter(s) in this box.

If you are enclosing a payment please tick this box. ✓

DECLARATION: You, or someone on your behalf, must sign below.

I, PETRA SMITH declare that the
(Full name of signatory in BLOCK LETTERS)
information given above is true and complete.

Signature P. Smith   Date 15/12 20 X7

A false declaration can result in prosecution.

Answer to Practice activity 25

The VAT return and the cash payment due must be delivered to HM Customs & Excise by the end of the month following the end of the VAT return period. So for this return the due date is 31 December 20X7.

Answer to Practice activity 26

Supplies made

The supplies made are as follows.

	Exempt £	*Zero rated* £	*Standard rated* £
	62,000	27,000	3,850
	35,250	33,500	11,250
	24,870	7,500	8,500
	1,800		
	32,000		
	155,920	68,000	23,600
VAT at 17.5%			4,130
			27,730

The total net amount is £247,520.

Answer to Practice activity 27

Supplies received

The supplies received are as follows.

	Car £	*Materials for self-supply* £	*Purchases for exempt supplies* £	*Other* £
Net	15,000	3,000	22,000	13,400
VAT	2,625	525	3,850	2,345
Gross	17,625	3,525	25,850	15,745

The total net amount is £53,400.

The total VAT incurred is £9,345.

Answer to Practice activity 28

Fuel for private use

The provision of fuel for the managing director's car gives rise to a deemed supply as follows.

	£
Net £325 × 40/47	276.60
VAT £325 × 7/47	48.40
	325.00

Answer to Practice activity 29

Understated output VAT

The previous period's understatement of output VAT, £870, does not exceed £2,000 so it should be adjusted for on the current period's return.

Answer to Practice activity 30

Self-supply of stationery

The self-supply of stationery gives rise to the following deemed supply by and to the company.

	£
Net	16,000
VAT at 17.5%	2,800
	18,800

Answer to Practice activity 31

The bad debts

Payments received, which are not in respect of particular invoices, are applied to debts in chronological order. The debts remaining unpaid are therefore as follows.

Due date	Amount £	Payment on 15.12.X2 £	Payment on 1.1.X3 £	Balance £	VAT at 7/47 £
1.3.X2	724	(724)		0	0.00
1.12.X2	830	(276)	(200)	354	52.72
1.3.X3	680			680	101.27
31.3.X3	520			520	77.44
10.6.X3	327			327	48.70

VAT of £52.72 can be reclaimed immediately under bad debt relief. The remaining VAT cannot be reclaimed until the relevant debts are over six months old (as measured from the due date for payment).

Answer to Practice activity 32

The recoverable input VAT is as follows.

	£
Car: none recoverable because some private use	0.00
Materials for self-supply	525.00
Purchase for exempt supplies: none recoverable	0.00
Other £(2,345 + 2,800) × 38%★	1,955.10
	2,480.10
Bad debt relief	52.72
	2,532.82

★The partial exemption calculation

The value of taxable supplies is £(68,000 + 23,600 + 227) = £91,877. Note that the deemed supply of fuel for private motoring is included, but the self-supply of stationery is excluded.

The value of all supplies is £(91,877 + 155,920) = £247,797.

The partial exemption fraction is 91,877/247,797 = 0.3707, rounded up to 38%.

Answer to Practice activity 33

The output VAT to account for is as follows.

	£
VAT on supplies	4,130.00
VAT on fuel for private use	48.40
VAT on self-supply	2,800.00
Error in previous period	870.00
	7,848.40

Answer to Practice activity 34

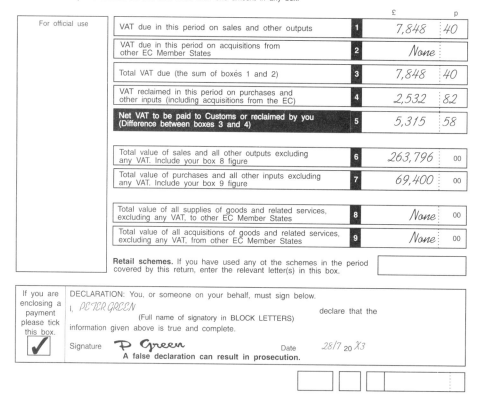

Value Added Tax Return
For the period
01 04 X3 to 30 06 X3

For Official Use

Registration number: 431 9824 79

Period: 06 X3

You could be liable to a financial penalty if your completed return and all the VAT payable are not received by the due date.

Due date: 31 07 X3

For Official Use

STRODE LTD
63 FIG STREET
TREETOWN
TR1 4NF

Your VAT Office telephone number is 0123-4567

Before you fill in this form please read the notes on the back and the VAT Leaflet *"Filling in your VAT return"*. Complete all boxes clearly in ink, and write 'none' where necessary. Don't put a dash or leave any box blank. If there are no pence write "00" in the pence column. Do not enter more than one amount in any box.

For official use			£	p
VAT due in this period on sales and other outputs	1		7,848	40
VAT due in this period on acquisitions from other EC Member States	2		None	
Total VAT due (the sum of boxes 1 and 2)	3		7,848	40
VAT reclaimed in this period on purchases and other inputs (including acquisitions from the EC)	4		2,532	82
Net VAT to be paid to Customs or reclaimed by you (Difference between boxes 3 and 4)	5		5,315	58
Total value of sales and all other outputs excluding any VAT. Include your box 8 figure	6		263,796	00
Total value of purchases and all other inputs excluding any VAT. Include your box 9 figure	7		69,400	00
Total value of all supplies of goods and related services, excluding any VAT, to other EC Member States	8		None	00
Total value of all acquisitions of goods and related services, excluding any VAT, from other EC Member States	9		None	00

Retail schemes. If you have used any of the schemes in the period covered by this return, enter the relevant letter(s) in this box.

If you are enclosing a payment please tick this box. ✓

DECLARATION: You, or someone on your behalf, must sign below.
I, PETER GREEN
(Full name of signatory in BLOCK LETTERS)
declare that the information given above is true and complete.

Signature P Green   Date 28/7 20 X3

A false declaration can result in prosecution.

Workings

The **total turnover** (Box 6) is £(247,520.00 + 276.60 + 16,000.00) = £263,796.60, rounded down to £263,796.

The **total purchases** (Box 7) are £(53,400 + 16,000)= £69,400.

Note: The £16,000 self supply is both an output and an input.

Answer to Practice activity 35

The claim for bad debt relief would be justified as follows.

(a) Amounts received (not specifically in respect of particular invoices) have been correctly allocated to debts in chronological order.

(b) The debts have been written off in the accounts.

(c) The only debt on which relief is now claimed dates back to a payment due on 1 December 20X2, which is more than six months ago.

(d) Records to show that the VAT on the supply was accounted for and the debt has been written off are held

(e) A copy of the original VAT invoice is held

(f) A notice has been sent to the debtor in question informing him that the debt has been the subject of a bad debt relief claim. This notice was sent within 7 days of making the claim. Included in the notice were details of which invoice the claim related to and the amount and date of the claim.

BPP
PUBLISHING

Answers to Practice Devolved Assessments

ANSWERS TO PRACTICE DEVOLVED ASSESSMENT 1: GRADY'S TUTORIAL COLLEGE

Tutorial note. Not many figures need to be entered on the ONS forms. However, the forms have quite lengthy accompanying notes. This highlights an important skill when completing reports and returns: to be able to review the information available in full and to select the information which is relevant to the task.

(a)   See the completed forms on pages 128 and 129.

Working

Total turnover is calculated as follows.

	£	£
College Division		
YTD 31.3.X4	583,636	
YTD 31.12.X3	(422,629)	
		161,007
Bookshop		
YTD 31.3.X4	71,094	
YTD 31.12.X3	(46,931)	
		24,163
Interdivisional (394 + 481 + 192)		(1,067)
		184,103

(b)   The return for the *Quarterly inquiry into turnover*, as stated in the ONS letter, should be returned within three weeks of the end of the period to which it relates. This period ends on 31 March 20X4 and so the form should be returned by 21 April 20X4.

The return for the *Quarterly inquiry into capital expenditure* should be returned by 14 April 20X4, as stated at the top of the form.

In view of these dates, neither form can wait for Kim's return from holiday and I would therefore take the following action.

(i)   Remind Kim of the dates by which the returns must be made and request that she be available to sign them before she leaves at 5.30 pm this evening.

(ii)   Make arrangements to complete the forms for signature today. The forms should be drafted by 4 pm at the latest, in case any changes are necessary following Kim's review of them.

Quarterly inquiry into turnover

IMPORTANT

Please read the notes before you fill in this form. Give the best estimates you can if you do not have exact figures.

FV			
T16/7704240000 72/112			

1. Details of business

Your business is classified as being in the industry described briefly in the letter accompanying this form. If you think this is wrong, please give a full description of your business. If you are involved in two or more activities, please describe the main one.

2. Period

Period for which you have filled in the form

	Day		Month		Year	
from	01	/	01	/	X4	11
to	31	/	03	/	X4	12

3. Turnover to the nearest £thousand (not including VAT)

Total turnover (including fees receivable)

184	40

4. Employees

Number of persons employed by the business at the end of the period covered by this return.

4.1   Total employees

13	50

of which

4.2	Full-time male	5	51
4.3	Part-time male	1	52
4.4	Full-time female	6	53
4.5	Part-time female	1	54

5. Other businesses included in this form

The form should be completed for the business named in the covering letter. If, exceptionally, you are unable to limit your return to the activities of this business, please list below the names and VAT registration numbers of the other businesses included.

Name of business   VAT registration number

....

....

(Please continue on a separate sheet if necessary)

REMARKS: If you have given any information which is significantly different from the last quarter, please explain.

PLEASE USE BLOCK CAPITALS

Name of person we should contact if necessary:	Kim Harvey	
Position in business:	Financial Controller	Date:	8/4/X4
Telephone no./ext:	020-7711 4240	Fax/Telex:	020-7711 4200

Quarterly inquiry into capital expenditure

PLEASE COMPLETE AND RETURN THIS FORM BY 14 APRIL 20X4

FV	93	Q1
8100/7104420000		

IMPORTANT   Please read the enclosed notes before completing this form. If you do not have precise figures available give the best estimates you can. All values should be shown to the nearest £ thousand

1.   PERIOD (see note 1)

Period covered by the return

		Day	Month	Year
from	08	31 /	01 /	X4
to	09	31 /	03 /	X4

2.   LAND AND BUILDINGS (see note 2)   £ thousand

2.1   New building work or other constructional work of a capital nature (excluding the cost of land and of new dwellings)

10	24

2.2   Acquisition of land and of existing buildings

20	32

2.3   Proceeds of land and buildings disposed of

30	NIL

3.   VEHICLES (see note 3)

3.1   New and second-hand acquisitions

40	10

3.2   Proceeds of vehicles disposed of

50	5

4.   PLANT, MACHINERY etc (see note 4)

4.1   New and second-hand acquisitions

60	4

4.2   Proceeds of plant, machinery etc disposed of

70	3

5.   TOTAL

5.1   Total acquisitions (2.1 + 2.2 + 3.1 + 4.1)

90	70

5.2   Total disposals (2.3 + 3.2 + 4.2)

100	8

6.   FINANCE LEASING

6.1   Total amount included in acquisitions at 2.1, 3.1 and 4.1 for assets leased under finance leasing arrangements.

80	NIL

7.   COMMENTS ON UNUSUAL FLUCTUATIONS IN FIGURES WOULD BE APPRECIATED

....

Name of person to be contacted if necessary............KIM HARVEY..................................
BLOCK CAPITALS PLEASE

Position in company...FINANCIAL CONTROLLER   Signature..

Telephone No/Ext......020-7711 4240................ Fax...020-7711 4200 Date...8 APRIL 20X4.....

(c)

Quarter to	31 Mar 20X4		31 Dec 20X3		30 Sept 20X3		30 June 20X3	
College Division	£'000	%	£'000	%	£'000	%	£'000	%
Turnover	161.0	100.0	152.8	100.0	145.1	100.0	124.7	100.0
Direct costs	(70.8)	(44.0)	(68.4)	(44.8)	(66.7)	(46.0)	(64.1)	(51.4)
Other operating costs	(24.6)	(15.3)	(29.4)	(19.2)	(21.5)	(14.8)	(22.0)	(17.6)
Contribution	65.6	40.7	55.0	36.0	56.9	39.2	38.6	31.0
Bookshop								
Turnover	24.2	100.0	18.7	100.0	15.5	100.0	12.7	100.0
Cost of sales	(15.2)		(11.9)		(9.6)		(8.1)	
Gross profit	9.0	37.2	6.8	36.4	5.9	38.1	4.6	36.2
Staff costs	(4.4)		(4.3)		(4.1)		(4.2)	
Other operating costs	(2.8)		(2.2)		(2.0)		(2.4)	
Contribution	1.8	7.4	0.3	1.6	(0.2)	(1.3)	(2.0)	(15.7)
Bookshop staff nos.	1.5		1.5		1.5		1.0	
Sales per staff member (£'000)	16.1		12.5		10.3		12.7	

(d) (i) *College Division*

Percentage of turnover

Quarter to	31 Mar 20X4	31 Dec 20X3	30 Sept 20X3	30 June 20X3
Direct costs	44.0	44.8	46.0	51.4
Other operating costs	15.3	19.,2	14.8	17.6
Contribution	40.7	36.0	39.2	31.0

(ii) *Bookshop*

Gross profit oercentage	40- 30- 20- 10- 0-	37.2	36.4	38.1	36.2

Quarter to	31 Mar 20X4	31 Dec 20X3	30 Sept 20X3	30 June 20X3

Sales per staff member (£'000)

	16.1	12.5	10.3	12.7

(e) The measurement of the productivity of the teaching staff requires the establishment of an appropriate unit to measure the output of teachers.

If records are kept of the number of hours of contact between students and staff, productivity could be measured as lecture hours per teacher or student contact hours per teacher, where student contact hours equals the number of students in a lecture multiplied by the length of the lecture. Such measures might be applied to the teaching staff overall or to individual teachers.

If we want to measure the quality of teachers' work more closely, we might use records of the grades obtained by students and weight the output of teachers according to the grades of their students, thus awarding different teachers scores according to the performance of their students. This measure will require records on student grades to be maintained, and it may be seen as unfair if different student groups have different ability ranges.

ANSWERS TO PRACTICE DEVOLVED ASSESSMENT 2: IRIS LTD

(a) *Information from the sales report*

Total sales, excluding VAT, are £1,044,980, and total VAT is £135,640.75.

The standard rated sales are £135,640.75/0.175 = £775,090.

The exempt sales are £(1,044,980 – 775,090) = £269,890.

Adjustments to the sales report figures

The sales of £16,000 invoiced in December but delivered in January must be added to the total of standard rated sales, and the sales of £24,600 delivered in September but invoiced in October must also be added. The adjusted figures are as follows.

Total sales: £(1,044,980 + 16,000 + 24,600) = £1,085,580

Standard rated sales: £(775,090 + 16,000 + 24,600) = £815,690

Output VAT: £815,690 × 17.5% = £142,745.75

Exempt sales: £269,890

Recoverable percentage of unattributed input VAT: £815,690/£1,085,580 = 75.1%, rounded up to 76%.

Purchases

Total purchases are £644,953, and the total VAT is £72,563.40.

Bad debt relief

The total amount owed by the customer in liquidation, including VAT, was £7,600 × 1.175 = £8,930. Of this, £5,930 is still owing.

The bad debt, including VAT, is £5,930 × 60% = £3,558.

The VAT in this amount is £3,558 × 7/47 = £529.91.

Recoverable input VAT

	£
Attributable to taxable supplies £72,563.40 × 45%	32,653.53
Unattributable £72,563.40 × 35% × 76%	19,301.86
	51,955.39
Bad debt relief	529.91
	52,485.30

The 'exempt input VAT' totals £20,608.01 (£72,563.40 – 32,653.53 – 19,301.86).

The '£625 a month on average' limit for exempt input VAT is clearly exceeded, so none of the exempt input VAT is recoverable.

The VAT return can now be completed.

Value Added Tax Return

For the period
01 10 X5 to 31 12 X5

For Official Use

Registration number

653 5306 77

Period

12 X5

You could be liable to a financial penalty if your completed return and all the VAT payable are not received by the due date.

IRIS LTD
1 FLOWER STREET
BLOOMTOWN
BL1 4LN

Due date: 31 01 X6

For Official Use

Your VAT Office telephone number is 0123-4567

Before you fill in this form please read the notes on the back and the VAT Leaflet *"Filling in your VAT return"*. Fill in all boxes clearly in ink, and write 'none' where necessary. Don't put a dash or leave any box blank. If there are no pence write "00" in the pence column. Do not enter more than one amount in any box.

For official use		£	p
	VAT due in this period on sales and other outputs **1**	142,745	75
	VAT due in this period on acquisitions from other EC Member States **2**	NONE	
	Total VAT due (the sum of boxes 1 and 2) **3**	142,745	75
	VAT reclaimed in this period on purchases and other inputs (including acquisitions from the EC) **4**	52,485	30
	Net VAT to be paid to Customs or reclaimed by you (Difference between boxes 3 and 4) **5**	90,260	45
	Total value of sales and all other outputs excluding any VAT. Include your box 8 figure **6**	1,085,580	00
	Total value of purchases and all other inputs excluding any VAT. Include your box 9 figure **7**	644,953	00
	Total value of all supplies of goods and related services, excluding any VAT, to other EC Member States **8**	NONE	00
	Total value of all acquisitions of goods and related services, excluding any VAT, from other EC Member States **9**	NONE	00

Retail schemes. If you have used any of the schemes in the period covered by this return, enter the relevant letter(s) in this box.

If you are enclosing a payment please tick this box. ✔

DECLARATION: You, or someone on your behalf, must sign below.
I, ANDREW TECH .... declare that the
(Full name of signatory in BLOCK LETTERS)
information given above is true and complete.
Signature... A Tech .... Date 30/01 20 X6
A false declaration can result in prosecution.

BPP PUBLISHING

(b)

DRAFT

Senior Accountant
Iris Ltd
Iris House
Coventry

HM Customs & Excise
Excise House
Coventry

12.01.20X6

Dear Sir

CONFERENCE COSTS

We are due to hold a conference next month in Birmingham and the costs duly incurred will include approximately £3,000 of input VAT. I am writing to you for guidance with respect to the deductibility of the input VAT incurred.

The aim of the conference is to promote the name and products of Iris Ltd and delegates at the conference will comprise potential customers, current suppliers and our sales team.

I enclose a copy of the quotation received from the venue but in summary the costs incurred comprise room hire, equipment hire (to allow the showing of several promotional films) and lunchtime food and drink. The conference will run from 11am to 4pm.

If you require any further information or wish to discuss anything in more detail please do not hesitate to contact me. I look forward to your reply.

Your faithfully

Mr Jay

Senior Accountant

(c)

MEMORANDUM

To: Finance Director
From: Accountant
Date: 29 January 20X6
Subject: Mistakes in VAT returns

Thank you for your memorandum dated 28 January.

(i)   If your friend makes errors on a VAT return, he can simply correct the error on a later return so long as the net error (error in output VAT net of error in input VAT) does not exceed £2,000. He should simply increase or reduce the figure in box 1, box 2 or box 4 as appropriate. If a figure becomes negative because of this, it should be shown in brackets.

Errors exceeding £2,000 net must be separately notified to the local VAT office.

(ii) There are two penalties for understatements of the amount of VAT due. They are the misdeclaration penalty for very large errors and the misdeclaration penalty for repeated errors.

The former penalty applies when the VAT which would have been lost equals or exceeds the lower of £1m or 30% of the sum of the correct input VAT and the correct output VAT.

The latter penalty applies when there is a series of material inaccuracies, (ie errors) when the VAT which would have been lost equals or exceeds the lower of £500,000 or 10% of the sum of the correct input VAT and the correct output VAT. The first material inaccuracy leads to a penalty period of eight VAT return periods starting. Any material inaccuracies in that period, apart from the first one, incur the penalty.

In both cases, the penalty is 15% of the VAT which would have been lost. If the penalty for very large errors applies to an error, the penalty for repeated errors cannot also apply but the error can lead to the start of a penalty period.

(d)

> ## MEMORANDUM
>
> To: Data Processing Manager
> From: Accountant
> Date: 29 January 20X6
> Subject: New accounting software – rounding of VAT
>
> Thank you for your memorandum dated 28 January. The rules on the rounding of amounts of VAT are as follows.
>
> (a)   If amounts of VAT are calculated for individual lines on an invoice, they must be:
>
>   (i)   rounded down to the nearest 0.1p, so 86.76p would be shown as 86.7p; or
>
>   (ii)   rounded to the nearest 0.5p, so 86.76p would be shown as 87p and 86.26p would be shown as 86.5p
>
> (b)   If amounts of VAT are calculated from an amount of VAT per unit or article, the amount of VAT should be:
>
>   (i)   calculated to the nearest 0.01p and then rounded to the nearest 0.1p, so 0.24p would be rounded to 0.2p; or
>
>   (ii)   rounded to the nearest 0.5p, but with a minimum of 0.5p for any standard rated item, so 0.24p would be rounded to 0.5p rather than to 0p.
>
> (c)   The total VAT shown on an invoice should be rounded down to the nearest 1p, so £32.439 would be shown as £32.43.

Answers to Trial Run Devolved Assessments

ANSWERS TO TRIAL RUN DEVOLVED ASSESSMENT 1: MYLLTON LTD

Task 1

1999	Monthly purchases at invoiced prices, including VAT £'000	Index of materials purchased by the Wood and Wood Products Industry, 1995 =100	Value of timber purchases at current prices, including VAT £'000
January	138	96.9	134
February	173	96.2	166
March	147	95.8	141
April	171	95.8	164
May	138	95.7	132
June	232	95.5	222
July	209	95.2	199
August	196	95.0	186
September	274	94.6	259
October	225	94.3	212
November	201	94.4	190
December	183	94.4	173
Total	2,287	na	2,178

Note. The precise total for the adjusted purchases, to the nearest £'000, is £2,177,000. The difference between this and the figure shown is caused by rounding the figures for each month in column three to the nearest £'000 before calculating the total. However, £2,178,000 is the figure required as it is obtained by complying with the instructions.

Task 2

	£'000
Value of timber purchases at current prices, including VAT	2,178
VAT included above at 17.5%	324
Value of timber purchases at current prices, excluding VAT	1,854

Task 3

MEMO

To: Romy Gurlane

From: Olivia Tran

Subject: Effect of Graviner Ltd's use of 1995 transfer prices for timber during 1999

Date: 2 August 2000

The table below sets out the comparative figures for 1999 that you requested.

	Using 1999 accounts	*Using current indexed values for timber purchased from Graviner Ltd*
Gross profit percentage	23%	26%
Net profit percentage	6%	8%
Return on capital employed (ROCE)	12%	16%

* ROCE = Net profit ÷ capital employed

Workings for Task 3

	Figures contained in 1999 accounts	*Figures using indexed value for timber purchased from Graviner*
	£'000	£'000
Sales	**4,264**	**4,264**
Timber purchases from Graviner	1,946	1,854
Other material purchases	328	328
Production labour	739	739
Production overheads	254	254
Gross profit	**997**	**1,089**
Administration overheads	476	476
Selling and distribution costs	198	198
Other non-production costs	57	57
Net profit	**266**	**358**
Fixed assets (net book value)	1,847	1,847
Current assets	638	638
Current liabilities	204	204
Capital employed	**2,281**	**2,281**

Task 4

Timber and Ancillary Trades Federation

Gloster House, 33 Loville Road, Dartford, Kent DA8 3QQ

TURNOVER AND COSTS RETURN 1999

Company or Business Name	Hexa-Gann Group Plc
Membership number	H920/58
Accounting year end date	31 December 1999
Period covered by figures, if less than one year	na
	£m
Turnover	15,738
Timber purchases	7,938
Production labour costs	1,999
Other production costs	1,177
Non-production costs	1,838
Total costs	12,952

Notes.
1. All figures should exclude VAT.
2. All figures should be to the nearest £100,000 and expressed as decimal millions (eg £31,832,420 would be £31.8)
3. This return should be signed by an officer of the company, or the owner or a partner if unincorporated.

Signature:

Name:

Position:

Date:

Please return to Annabelle Peruke at the above address by 6 August 2000, marked 'Private & Confidential'.

Workings for Task 4

	Graviner Ltd £'000	Myllton Ltd £'000	Total £'000
Sales (including sales to other members of the Hexa-Gann Group)	13,420	4,264	
Less sales to Myllton Ltd		1,946	
Net sales	**13,420**	**2,318**	**15,738**
Timber purchases (all from outside the Hexa-Gann Group)	**7,938**		**7,938**
Production labour costs	**1,260**	**739**	**1,999**
Other material purchases	276	328	
Production overheads	319	254	
Other production costs	**595**	**582**	**1,177**
Administration overheads	684	476	
Selling and distribution costs	276	198	
Other non-production costs	147	57	
Non-production costs	**1107**	**731**	**1,838**
Total costs	**10,900**	**2,052**	**12,952**

Task 5

MEMO

To: Nigel Lyte

From: Olivia Tran

Subject: TATF Turnover and Costs Return 1999

Date: 2 August 2000

I enclose the above return , duly completed, for your authorisation prior to despatch.

Please note that the due date for its return to the TATF is Friday 6 August. May I please have your authorisation to send it by Special Delivery.

Task 6

MYLLTON LTD			
PRODUCTIVITY REPORT			
Period	Standard Hours produced (3 month total)	Production labour hours worked (3 month total)	Output hours per input hour
March 00 to May 00	20,280	21,311	0.952
April 00 to June 00	19,915	20,715	0.961
May 00 to July 00	21,340	21,630	0.987

Task 7

Value Added Tax Return

For the period
01 05 00 to 31 07 00

For Official Use

Registration number   Period

| 578 4060 20 | 07 00 |

You could be liable to a financial penalty if your completed return and all the VAT payable are not received by the due date.

| 081 578 4060 19 100 03 98   Q35192 |

Due date: 31 08 00

James Mbanu
Myllton Ltd
23 Cavour Road
Bridge Trading Estate
New Sarum SPO 7YT   219921/10

| For Official Use | |

Your VAT Office telephone number is 01682-386000

Before you fill in this form please read the notes on the back and the VAT Leaflet *"Filling in your VAT return"*. Fill in all boxes clearly in ink, and write 'none' where necessary. Don't put a dash or leave any box blank. If there are no pence write "00" in the pence column. Do not enter more than one amount in any box.

			£	p
For official use	VAT due in this period on sales and other outputs	**1**	186,607	34
	VAT due in this period on acquisitions from other EC Member States	**2**	2,291	54
	Total VAT due (the sum of boxes 1 and 2)	**3**	188,898	88
	VAT reclaimed in this period on purchases and other inputs (including acquisitions from the EC)	**4**	103,524	83
	Net VAT to be paid to Customs or reclaimed by you (Difference between boxes 3 and 4)	**5**	85,374	05
	Total value of sales and all other outputs excluding any VAT. Include your box 8 figure	**6**	1,066,327	00
	Total value of purchases and all other inputs excluding any VAT. Include your box 9 figure	**7**	716,250	00
	Total value of all supplies of goods and related services, excluding any VAT, to other EC Member States	**8**	Nil	00
	Total value of all acquisitions of goods and related services, excluding any VAT, from other EC Member States	**9**	13,094	00

Retail schemes. If you have used any ot the schemes in the period covered by this return, enter the relevant letter(s) in this box.

If you are enclosing a payment please tick this box. [✓]

DECLARATION: You, or someone on your behalf, must sign below.
I, **James Mbanu** .... declare that the
(Full name of signatory in BLOCK LETTERS)
information given above is true and complete.

Signature.. Date **2 Aug** 20 **00**
A false declaration can result in prosecution.

B

0196929   PCU(November 1995)

VAT 100 (Half)

Calculations for Box 4

		£
VAT on purchases from UK suppliers		105,473.43
less	VAT on car purchased (not exclusively for business use)	(4,978.90)
plus	VAT on acquisions from EC member states (Box 2)	2,291.54
plus	VAT bad debt relief being claimed	738.76
		103,524.83

BPP
PUBLISHING

Task 8

MYLLTON LTD

23 Cavour Road, Bridge Trading Estate, New Sarum SPO 7YT
Telephone 01722-883567

HM Customs & Excise
Roebuck House
24-28 Bedford Place
Southampton SO15 2DB

2 August 2000

Dear Sirs,

Registration number: 578 4060 20

The company is proposing to host a canal boat evening during August 2000 for its staff and representatives of its customers. An evening meal will be provided, together with music and a free bar. This is a standard package supplied by Knet Cruises Ltd, who are registered for VAT.

As VAT can only be reclaimed in respect of staff entertainment we are not clear as to how the VAT element of the supplier's invoice should be treated.

I would welcome your advice as to the correct treatment for VAT purposes of this supply.

Yours faithfully

Olivia Tran
Deputy Accountant

Registered office: 23 Cavour Road, Bridge Trading Estate, New Sarum SPO 7YT
Registered in England, number 2314562

ANSWERS TO TRIAL RUN DEVOLVED ASSESSMENT 2: LANBERGIS HIRE LTD

Task 1

Calculation of Vehicle running costs index

| | Year | 1999 | 1999 | 1999 | 1999 | 2000 | 2000 | 2000 | 2000 |
	Month	Sep	Oct	Nov	Dec	Jan	Feb	Mar	Apr
Maintenance of motor vehicles	Index multiplied by weight ie 23	4,526.4	4,531.0	4,531.0	4,540.2	4,563.2	4,570.1	4,590.8	4,616.1
Vehicle tax and insurance	Index multiplied by weight ie 20	4,266.0	4,226.0	4,226.0	4,226.0	4,350.0	4,350.0	4,400.0	4,498.0
Total		8,792.4	8,757.0	8,757.0	8,766.2	8,913.2	8,920.1	8,990.8	9,114.1

The above total divided by the sum of the weights, ie 43, gives the vehicle running costs index

Vehicle running costs index (13 January 1988 = 100)

Year	1999	1999	1999	1999	2000	2000	2000	2000
Month	Sep	Oct	Nov	Dec	Jan	Feb	Mar	Apr
Vehicle running costs index	204.5	203.7	203.7	203.9	207.3	207.4	209.1	212.0

Task 2

Re-basing of Purchase of motor vehicles index and Vehicle running costs index to September 1999 = 100

Year	1999	1999	1999	1999	2000	2000	2000	2000
Month	Sep	Oct	Nov	Dec	Jan	Feb	Mar	Apr
Purchase of motor vehicles index (13 Jan 1998 = 100)	139.2	137.9	136.6	134.6	137.1	137.0	136.8	137.1
Vehicle running costs index (13 Jan 1998 = 100)	204.5	203.7	203.7	203.9	207.3	207.4	209.1	212.0

Re-basing is achieved by multiplying the index for each month by 100 and dividing the result by the index for the base period, eg $(137.9 \times 100) \div 139.2 = 99.1$

Purchase of motor vehicles index and Vehicle running costs index
Re-based to September 1999 = 100

Year	1999	1999	1999	1999	2000	2000	2000	2000
Month	Sep	Oct	Nov	Dec	Jan	Feb	Mar	Apr
Purchase of motor vehicles index (Sep 1999 = 100)	100.0	99.1	98.1	96.7	98.5	98.4	98.3	98.5
Vehicle running costs index (Sep 1999 = 100)	100.0	99.6	99.6	99.7	101.4	101.4	102.2	103.7

Task 3

MEMO

To: Raju Shah

From: Eric Kendall

Subject: Changes in UK motoring costs since September 1999

Date: 16 August 2000

You asked me to investigate the changes in UK motoring costs since the last change in the company's prices in September 1999. I was asked to produce separate figures for running costs and for car purchase prices. This information will be compared with the changes in Lanbergis Hire Ltd's operating costs.

As a first step I referred to the motoring expenditure price index contained in the June 2000 edition of the Monthly Digest of Statistics. However, this index is not entirely suitable.

1. It contains expenditure on petrol and oil, whereas Lanbergis Hire Ltd's customers pay for all petrol consumed.
2. The weights used to the combine mix of motoring costs may not be in the same proportions as Lanbergis Hire Ltd's costs[1].

As a second step I combined the index for maintenance of motor vehicles with that for vehicle tax and insurance, to produce an index of vehicle running costs which excludes the costs of petrol and oil.

The third step was to re-base this index and that for the purchase prices of motor vehicles, using September 1999 as the base period (index = 100).

The results are shown in the table attached to this report. Particular points to note are that the index for purchase prices of vehicles has dropped by 1.5%, whereas the index for vehicle running costs has increased by 3.7% over the period.

It would be possible to construct a single index from the components of the motoring expenditure price index which would reflect the makeup of Lanbergis Hire Ltd's costs more accurately. This could be done by combining the index of vehicle running costs with that for purchase prices of vehicles which are contained in the attached table. They could be combined by using the relative weights contained in the Retail Prices Index.[2]

Eric Kendall

Notes.

1.   An alternative could be the fact that the index does not contain an element which would reflect Lanbergis Hire Ltd's administration costs.

2.   Alternatively, Lanbergis Hire Ltd's own cost structure could be used to provide the weights. This would provide a better comparison than using the private household weights contained in the Retail Prices Index.

BPP
PUBLISHING

Task 4

Kirkmanor District Council
Environmental Services Department
Town Hall, Kirkmanor XA3 9RS

Value Added Questionnaire - Strictly Confidential

The following information is required to enable the charge for the collection of industrial and commercial waste to be calculated. Failure to reply within 60 days of the designated period end will result in an estimated charge which may exceed considerably that which would normally be payable.

Where waste from more than one business is collected from the same location it will be necessary to consolidate the figures for all businesses operating from that location.

This questionnaire must be completed twice per calendar year, in respect of the six-month period ending 30 June and again in respect of the six month period ending 31 December. In the case of commencement or cessation of a business the questionnaire should be completed to or from the half-year date closest to the date of commencement or cessation.

Company or Business Name(s)	Lanbergis Hire Ltd Outcastle Auto Ltd
Full postal address of location from which waste is collected.	71 Marefair Lanbergis Outcastle XA32 7DD
Period covered by this questionnaire	01 January 2000 to 30 June 2000
Turnover, excluding VAT	£ 2,673,586
Value added	£ 1,122,415

For the purposes of this questionnaire
- *Turnover* should exclude the proceeds from the disposal of capital goods, land and buildings, and all transactions between businesses operating from the same location.
- *Capital goods* are defined as fixed assets which are eligible for capital allowances in the calculation of income tax or corporation tax.
- *Value added* is defined as Turnover, excluding VAT, less Purchased Inputs excluding VAT.
- *Purchased inputs* should exclude purchases of capital goods, land and buildings and transactions between businesses operating from the same location.

Signature of authorised person	Date: 16 August 2000
Name Raju Shah	Position: Managing Director, Lanbergis Hire Ltd.

The information contained in this questionnaire is confidential and will not be used for any other purpose.

Workings for Task 4

Calculation of 'turnover'

	Lanbergis Hire Ltd	Outcastle Auto Ltd	Total
	£	£	£
Given turnover figures	1,427,602	1,398,717	
Less			
Inter-company sales included in turnover	18,376	43,524	
Disposals of capital goods included in turnover	89,320	1,513	
Adjusted turnover	1,319,906	1,353,680	2,673,586

Calculation of 'purchased inputs'

	Lanbergis Hire Ltd	Outcastle Auto Ltd	Total
	£	£	£
Purchases of goods and services, including inter-company transactions	1,042,836	972,374	
Less			
Inter-company transactions included in purchases.	43,524	18,376	
Purchases of capital goods included in 'purchases of goods and services'	382,718	19,421	
Purchased inputs	616,594	934,577	1,551,171

Calculation of 'value added'

Combined adjusted turnover £2,673,586 less purchase inputs £1,551,171 = 'value added' £1,122,415.

Note.
The methods used to calculate 'value added' in this Assessment are not suitable for general application.

Task 5

MEMO

To: Raju Shah

From: Eric Kendall

Subject: Kirkmanor District Council value added questionnaire.

Date: 16 August 2000

I attach the completed value added questionnaire required by Kirkmanor District Council in respect of the six-month period ending 30 June 2000.

The questionnaire is to be returned by 30 August 2000.

May I have your signature on the questionnaire as authority to despatch it.

Eric Kendall

Task 6

LANBERGIS HIRE LTD

VEHICLE UTILISATION REPORT

WEEK ENDING Sunday 15 August 2000

1. Car-days in company ownership	527
2. Car-days unavailable due to servicing & repairs	25
3. Car-days available for hire or leasing (1 minus 2)	502
4. Availability percentage (3 as % of 1)	95.3%
5. Car-days on long-term leases	132
6. Car-days on short-term rentals	329
7. Car-days hired out or leased (5 plus 6)	461
8. Hire-days percentage (7 as % of 3)	91.8%
Report completed by: *Eric Kendall*	Date: 16 August 2000

Notes.
1. The percentages are to be expressed to one decimal place.
2. Do not use fractions of days. Events occurring before midday are treated as occurring at 00.01 hours. Events occurring after midday are treated as occurring at 24.00 hours.

Workings for Task 6

1. *Car-days in company ownership*

	72	at beginning of week	x	7	=	504
less	1	car written off Tues pm	x	5	=	(5)
add	6	cars delivered Tues am	x	6	=	36
less	4	cars sold Friday pm	x	2	=	(8)
						527

2. *Car-days unavailable due to servicing and repairs*

1	breakdown Wed am	x	5	=	5
6	pre-hire service, Tues/Wed	x	2	=	12
4	pre-sale cleaning, Thur/Fri	x	2	=	8
					25

3. *Car-days available for hiring or leasing* = 527   -   25   =   502

4. *Availability percentage* = (502×100) ÷   527   =   95.3%

5. *Car-days on long-term leases*

	16	for whole week	x	7	=	112
less	1	returned on Wednesday pm	x	4	=	(4)
add	6	leased out on Thursday am	x	4	=	24
						132

6. *Car-days on short-term rentals*

33	x	1	=	33
34	x	2	=	68
15	x	3	=	45
8	x	4	=	32
4	x	5	=	20
2	x	6	=	12
17	x	7	=	119
				329

7. *Car-days hired out or leased* = 132   +   329   =   461

8. *Hire-days percentage* = (461×100) ÷   502   =   91.8%

Task 7

Lanbergis Hire Ltd
71 Marefair, Lanbergis Outcastle XA32 7DD
Telephone 01898-883567

H M Customs & Excise
2nd Floor
Tower Chambers
31 Skew Road
Kirkmanor XA3 9TY

16 August 2000

Dear Sirs,

Registration Number 578 4060 21

Lanbergis Hire Ltd has a car belonging to Harller AB, a Swedish company, which was left in its possession by a customer of Harller AB, on 7 August 2000. Normal practice would be to return the vehicle directly to Harller AB in Sweden at a cost of £800.

Cary Levinson, a salesman employed by San Luis Exchange Inc., an American company, has agreed to deliver the car back to Harller AB during a sales tour of Scandinavia that he will be making in the near future, instead of renting a car from Lanbergis Hire Ltd.

Mr Levinson intends to take possession of the car on 18 August 2000 so that he may use it during a holiday in Scotland. He will then use the car while visiting clients in Britain and Scandinavia.

Two alternative ways of charging for this are being considered.

1. Lanbergis Hire Ltd to charge San Luis Exchange Inc. £1,000, and San Luis Exchange Inc. to charge Harller AB £800
2. Lanbergis Hire Ltd to charge Harller AB £800 and San Luis Exchange Inc. £200.

It would be left to San Luis Exchange Inc., in either case, to recover the value of the private use from Mr Levinson if the company wished.

Would you please advise me of the correct VAT treatment for Lanbergis Hire Ltd to adopt in each case.

Yours faithfully

Eric Kendall

Eric Kendall
Acting Accountant

Registered office: 71 Marefair, Lanbergis Outcastle XA32 7DD
Registered in England, number 2314563

Task 8

Value Added Tax Return
For the period
01 05 00 to 31 07 00

For Official Use

Registration number	Period
578 4060 21	07 00

You could be liable to a financial penalty if your completed return and all the VAT payable are not received by the due date.

081 578 4060 19 100 03 98   Q35192

Barbara Mandeville
Lanbergis Ltd
71 Marefair
Lanbergis Outcastle
XA32 7DD   219921/10

Due date: 31 08 00

For Official Use

Your VAT Office telephone number is 01682-386000

Before you fill in this form please read the notes on the back and the VAT Leaflet *"Filling in your VAT return"*. Fill in all boxes clearly in ink, and write 'none' where necessary. Don't put a dash or leave any box blank. If there are no pence write "00" in the pence column. Do not enter more than one amount in any box.

		£	p
For official use	VAT due in this period on sales and other outputs	**1**	263,654	69
	VAT due in this period on acquisitions from other EC Member States	**2**	-	
	Total VAT due (the sum of boxes 1 and 2)	**3**	263,654	69
	VAT reclaimed in this period on purchases and other inputs (including acquisitions from the EC)	**4**	178,931	37
	Net VAT to be paid to Customs or reclaimed by you (Difference between boxes 3 and 4)	**5**	84,723	32
	Total value of sales and all other outputs excluding any VAT. Include your box 8 figure	**6**	1,506,598	00
	Total value of purchases and all other inputs excluding any VAT. Include your box 9 figure	**7**	1,161,319	00
	Total value of all supplies of goods and related services, excluding any VAT, to other EC Member States	**8**	-	00
	Total value of all acquisitions of goods and related services, excluding any VAT, from other EC Member States	**9**	-	00

Retail schemes. If you have used any of the schemes in the period covered by this return, enter the relevant letter(s) in this box.

If you are enclosing a payment please tick this box.

✓

DECLARATION: You, or someone on your behalf, must sign below.

I, **BARBARA MANDEVILLE** .... declare that the
(Full name of signatory in BLOCK LETTERS)
information given above is true and complete.

Signature... Date 23 Aug 20 00

A false declaration can result in prosecution.

B

0196929   PCU(November 1995)

VAT 100 (Half)

Workings for Task 8

	Lanbergis Hire Ltd £	Outcastle Auto Ltd £	Group return figures £
Given turnover, excluding VAT	815,928.42	699,358.57	
Less			
Inter-company sales included in turnover	12,736.00	28,452.75	
Plus			
Disposals of cars, excluding VAT, not included in turnover[1]	32,500.00		
Total value of sales and other outputs excluding any VAT	835,692.42	670,905.82	
Box 6 on VAT Return			1,506,598.24
VAT due this period on sales and other outputs[2]			
Box 1 on VAT Return			263,654.69
Purchases, including inter-company transactions, exc. VAT	494,814.67	476,781.92	
Plus			
Cars purchased, excluding VAT, not included in 'purchases'	189,723.00		
Total value of purchases and all other inputs exc. any VAT	684,537.67	476,781.92	
Box 7 on VAT Return			1,161,319.59
VAT on purchases other than cars.	74,212.70	71,517.15	
Plus			
VAT on cars purchased.[3]	33,201.52		
VAT reclaimed this period on purchases and other inputs	107,414.22	71,517.15	
Box 4 on VAT Return			178,931.37

Notes.
1. £38,187.50 ÷ 1.175
2. £1,506,598.24 × 0.175
3. £189,723 × 0.175

Answers to AAT Sample Simulation

ANSWERS TO AAT SAMPLE SIMULATION: HODDLE LTD

Task 1

Engineering Supplies Limited invoice

This is a valid VAT-only invoice. It should be processed as a March input and the VAT should be reclaimed in the quarter January to March 2000.

Alpha Stationery invoice

This is a valid VAT invoice of the less detailed kind. It should be processed as a March input and the VAT should be reclaimed in the quarter January to March 2000.

Jamieson & Co invoice

This is merely a proforma invoice. The service provided by Jamieson & Co cannot be regarded as an input until a valid invoice is received. The VAT should not be reclaimed at this stage.

Task 2

Value Added Tax Return

For the period
01 01 00 **to** 31 03 00

For Official Use

Registration number	Period
578 4060 19	03 00

081 578 4060 19 100 03 98   Q35192
MR SHERRY TEDDINGHAM
HODDLE LIMITED
22 FORMGUARD STREET
PEXLEY
PY6 3QW
219921/10

Due date: 31 04 00

For Official Use	

Your VAT Office telephone number is 01682 386000

ATTENTION
If this return and any tax due
are not received by the due date
you will be liable to a surcharge.

If you are using Retail Scheme B1, D or J,
please remember to carry out your annual
adjustment at the appropriate time.

Before you fill in this form please read the notes on the back and the VAT Leaflet *"Filling in your VAT return"*.
Fill in all boxes clearly in ink, and write 'none' where necessary. Don't put a dash or leave any box blank. If there are no pence
write "00" in the pence column. Do not enter more than one amount in any box.

For official use			£	p
	VAT due in this period on sales and other outputs	**1**	7,740	12
	VAT due in this period on acquisitions from other EU Member States	**2**	NONE	
	Total VAT due (the sum of boxes 1 and 2)	**3**	7,740	12
	VAT reclaimed in this period on purchases and other inputs (including acquisitions from the EU)	**4**	13,477	96
	Net VAT to be paid to Customs or reclaimed by you (Difference between boxes 3 and 4)	**5**	(5,737	84)
	Total value of sales and all other outputs excluding any VAT. Include your box 8 figure	**6**	120,606	00
	Total value of purchases and all other inputs excluding any VAT. Include your box 9 figure	**7**	80,727	00
	Total value of all supplies of goods and related services, excluding any VAT, to other EU Member States	**8**	10,870	00
	Total value of all acquisitions of goods and related services, excluding any VAT, from other EU Member States	**9**	NONE	00

Retail schemes. If you have used any of the schemes in the period
covered by this return, enter the relevant letter(s) in this box.

If you are enclosing a payment please tick this box. ✓

DECLARATION: You, or someone on your behalf, must sign below.
I, ... *SHERRY TEDDINGHAM* ..... declare that the
(Full name of signatory in BLOCK LETTERS)
information given above is true and complete.

Signature .... Date *9 April* 20 00
A false declaration can result in prosecution.

B

0196929   PCU(November 1995)

VAT 100 (Half)

*See page 168 for workings

Task 3

HODDLE LIMITED

22 Formguard Street, Pexley PY6 3QW
Telephone 01682 431 432256

9 April 2000

HM Customs & Excise
Brendon House
14 Abbey Street
Pexley PY2 3WR

Dear Sirs

Registration number: 578 4060 19

The company at present accounts for VAT on the basis of invoices raised and received. We are considering the idea of changing to the cash accounting scheme, and I would be grateful if you could provide some information on this. Perhaps there is a leaflet setting out details of the scheme?

The particular points of which we are uncertain are as follows.

- What turnover limits apply to the scheme? Are these limits affected by the fact that this company is part of a group consisting of the company itself and its parent company?

- How are bad debts accounted for under the cash accounting scheme?

I would be grateful for any assistance you are able to give on these points and generally about the workings of the scheme.

Yours faithfully

Sherry Teddingham

ACCOUNTANT

Registered office: 22 Formguard Street, Pexley PY6 3QW
Registered in England, number 2314561

Task 4

CONSOLIDATED PROFIT AND LOSS ACCOUNT
FOR THE THREE MONTHS ENDED 31 MARCH 2000

	Kelly £	*Hoddle* £	*Adjustments* £	*Consolidated* £
Sales	295,768	120,607	20,167	396,208
Opening stock	28,341	14,638		42,979
Purchases	136,095	50,908	18,271	168,732
	164,436	65,546		211,711
Closing stock	31,207	16,052	1,896	49,155
Cost of sales	133,229	*49,494		162,556
Gross profit	162,539	71,113		233,652
Wages and salaries	47,918	18,014		65,932
Distribution expenses	28,341	13,212		41,553
Administration expenses	30,189	11,676		41,865
Stationery	2,541	*544		3,085
Travel	2,001	267		2,268
Office expenses	3,908	737		4,645
Interest payable	12,017			12,017
Other expenses	11,765	3,384		15,149
	138,680	47,834		186,514
Net profit for the period	23,859	23,279		47,138

* See page 168 for workings.

Task 4

Tutorial note. You did not have to fill in the figures on this schedule but you would probably have found it helpful to do so.

**QUARTERLY CONSOLIDATED PROFIT AND LOSS ACCOUNTS
FOR THE YEAR ENDED 31 MARCH 2000**

	1 April 1999 - 30 June 1999 £	1 July 1999 - 30 September 1999 £	1 October 1999 - 31 December 1999 £	1 January 2000 - 31 March 2000 £	1 April 1999 - 31 March 2000 £
Sales	325,719	275,230	306,321	396,208	1,303,478
Cost of sales	134,861	109,421	121,358	162,556	528,196
Gross profit	190,858	165,809	184,963	233,652	775,282
Wages and salaries	63,314	61,167	64,412	65,932	254,825
Distribution expenses	34,217	30,135	31,221	41,553	137,126
Administration expenses	34,765	33,012	36,415	41,865	146,057
Stationery	2,981	2,671	3,008	3,085	11,745
Travel	1,975	1,876	2,413	2,268	8,532
Office expenses	4,412	4,713	3,083	4,645	16,853
Interest payable	12,913	12,714	12,432	12,017	50,076
Other expenses	10,981	16,421	15,431	15,149	57,982
	165,558	162,709	168,415	186,514	683,196
Net profit for the period	25,300	3,100	16,548	47,138	92,086

REPORT

To: Sherry Teddingham
From: Sol Bellcamp
Subject: Report on group results for the year ended 31 March 1999
Date: 9 April 2000

Introduction

This report contains the usual information on group results for the year, plus the additional information requested in your memo to me of 2 April 2000.

Key ratios

Gross profit margin = £775,282 ÷ £1,303,478 = 59.5%
Net profit margin = £92,086 ÷ £1,303,478 = 7.1%
Return on shareholders' capital employed = £92,086 ÷ £1,034,708 = 8.9%

Sales revenue by quarter

Quarter	Indexed	Indexed (base period = first quarter 1998/99)
	£	£
Apr - June 1999	325,719	315,511
Jul - Sep 1999	275,230	264,175
Oct - Dec 1999	306,321	291,005
Jan - Mar 2000	396,208	379,822

Pie chart showing sales by quarter

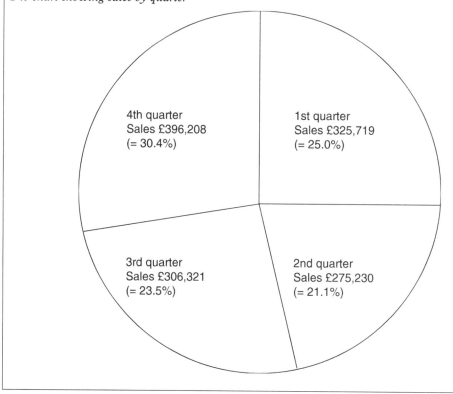

Task 6

INTERFIRM COMPARISON DATA (extracts)

Name of company...... Kelly Limited and subsidiary ......

Year ended .... 31 March 2000 ......

Data

	£	% of sales	*Industry best*	*Industry average*
Sales	1,303,478			
Gross profit	775,282	59.5%	62.1%	57.3%
Net profit	92,086	7.1%	10.4%	5.8%
Fixed assets	1,229,348			
Current assets	325,703			
Current liabilities	148,271			
Return on capital employed		10.1%	10.3%	9.0%

Task 7

MEMO

To: Sherry Teddingham

From: Sol Bellcamp

Subject: Interfirm comparison data

Date: 9 April 2000

I enclose the completed interfirm comparison data for the year ended 31 March 2000. Please let me know if you disagree with anything in it; otherwise, it is ready for despatch subject to your authorisation.

Workings

Task 2

		£
Box 4	PDB	12,690.53
	Petty cash	244.95
	Bad debt	73.50
	Engineering Supplies invoice	466.77
	Alpha Stationery invoice	2.21
		13,477.96
Box 7	PDB	79,179.67
	Petty cash	1,535.34
	Alpha Stationery invoice	12.63
		80,727.64

Task 4

Hoddle's cost of sales, January - March 2000

	£
Opening stock	14,638.00
Purchases	50,908.21
	65,546.21
Closing stock	16,052.00
Cost of sales	49,494.21

Hoddle's stationery costs, January - March 2000

	£
Petty cash book	531.55
Alpha Stationery sinvoice	12.63
	544.18

168

1.   Preparation of a financial statement (tabulating data)

2.   Preparation of a piechart

3.   Preparation of a bar chart

4.   Key financial ratios (calculation of)

5.   Graphs/charts

6.   Table

7.   Statement estimating annual income and costs

8.   Index numbers

9.   Compound bar chart

10.   Form

11.   ONS form

12.   Key performance ratios

13.   Table (comparison)

14.   Component bar chart

15.   Table

16.   Index numbers

17.   VAT errors

18.   Output VAT

19.   Input VAT

20.   Total net turnover calculation

21.   Total net purchases calculation

22.   VAT errors

23.   VAT account

24.   VAT return - preparation

25.   VAT return - dates

26.   VAT on supplies made

27.   VAT on supplies received

28.   VAT on fuel for private use

29.   Treatment of VAT errors in previous accounting periods

30.   Self-supply

31.   Bad debt relief

32.   Input VAT calculation

33.   Output VAT calculation

34.   VAT return - preparation

35.   Bad debt relief

BPP
PUBLISHING

ORDER FORM

Any books from our AAT range can be ordered by telephoning 020-8740-2211. Alternatively, send this page to our address below, fax it to us on 020-8740-1184, or email us at **publishing@bpp.com.** Or look us up on our website: www.bpp.com

We aim to deliver to all UK addresses inside 5 working days; a signature will be required. Order to all EU addresses should be delivered within 6 working days. All other orders to overseas addresses should be delivered within 8 working days.

To: BPP Publishing Ltd, Aldine House, Aldine Place, London W12 8AW

Tel: 020-8740 2211   **Fax: 020-8740 1184**   **Email: publishing@bpp.com**

Mr / Ms (full name): _____

Daytime delivery address: _____

_____

Postcode: _____   Daytime Tel: _____

Please send me the following quantities of books.

	5/00 Interactive Text	8/00 DA Kit	8/00 CA Kit
FOUNDATION			
Unit 1 Recording Income and Receipts (7/00 Text)	☐	☐	
Unit 2 Making and Recording Payments (7/00 Text)	☐		☐
Unit 3 Ledger Balances and Initial Trial Balance (7/00 Text)	☐	☐	
Unit 4 Supplying information for Management Control (6/00 Text)	☐		
Unit 20 Working with Information Technology (8/00 Text)	☐		
Unit 22/23 Achieving Personal Effectiveness (7/00) Text	☐		
INTERMEDIATE			
Unit 5 Financial Records and Accounts	☐		
Unit 6 Cost Information	☐	☐	
Unit 7 Reports and Returns	☐		
Unit 21 Using Information Technology	☐		
Unit 22: see below			
TECHNICIAN			
Unit 8/9 Core Managing Costs and Allocating Resources	☐		☐
Unit 10 Core Managing Accounting Systems	☐	☐	
Unit 11 Option Financial Statements (Accounting Practice)	☐		☐
Unit 12 Option Financial Statements (Central Government)	☐		
Unit 15 Option Cash Management and Credit Control	☐	☐	
Unit 16 Option Evaluating Activities	☐		
Unit 17 Option Implementing Auditing Procedures	☐		
Unit 18 Option Business Tax FA00(8/00 Text)	☐		
Unit 19 Option Personal Tax FA00(8/00 Text)	☐		
TECHNICIAN 1999			
Unit 17 Option Business Tax Computations FA99 (8/99 Text & Kit)	☐	☐	
Unit 18 Option Personal Tax Computations FA99 (8/99 Text & Kit)	☐		

TOTAL BOOKS   ☐ + ☐ + ☐ = ☐

@ £9.95 each = £ ☐

Postage and packaging:

UK: £2.00 for each book to maximum of £10

Europe (inc ROI and Channel Islands): £4.00 for first book, £2.00 for each extra

Rest of the World: £20.00 for first book, £10 for each extra

P & P   £ ☐

Unit 22 Maintaining a Healthy Workplace Interactive Text (postage free)   ☐ @ £3.95   £ ☐

GRAND TOTAL £ ☐

I enclose a cheque for £ _____ (cheques to **BPP Publishing Ltd**) or charge to **Mastercard/Visa/Switch**

Card number ☐☐☐☐ ☐☐☐☐ ☐☐☐☐ ☐☐☐☐ ☐☐☐☐

Start date _____   **Expiry date** _____   **Issue no. (Switch only)**___

Signature _____

REVIEW FORM & FREE PRIZE DRAW

All original review forms from the entire BPP range, completed with genuine comments, will be entered into one of two draws on 31 January 2001 and 31 July 2001. The names on the first four forms picked out on each occasion will be sent a cheque for £50.

Name: _____   Address: _____

_____

_____

How have you used this Devolved Assessment Kit?
(Tick one box only)

☐ Home study (book only)

☐ On a course: college _____

☐ With 'correspondence' package

☐ Other _____

Why did you decide to purchase this Devolved Assessment Kit? *(Tick one box only)*

☐ Have used BPP Texts in the past

☐ Recommendation by friend/colleague

☐ Recommendation by a lecturer at college

☐ Saw advertising

☐ Other _____

During the past six months do you recall seeing/receiving any of the following?
(Tick as many boxes as are relevant)

☐ Our advertisement in *Accounting Technician* magazine

☐ Our advertisement in *Pass*

☐ Our brochure with a letter through the post

Which (if any) aspects of our advertising do you find useful?
(Tick as many boxes as are relevant)

☐ Prices and publication dates of new editions

☐ Information on Interactive Text content

☐ Facility to order books off-the-page

☐ None of the above

Have you used the Interactive Text for this subject?   Yes ☐   No ☐

Your ratings, comments and suggestions would be appreciated on the following areas

	Very useful	Useful	Not useful
Introductory section (How to use this Devolved Assessment Kit etc)	☐	☐	☐
Practice Activities	☐	☐	☐
Practice Devolved Assessments	☐	☐	☐
Trial Run Devolved Assessments	☐	☐	☐
AAT Sample Simulation	☐	☐	☐
Content of Answers	☐	☐	☐
Layout of pages	☐	☐	☐
Structure of book and ease of use	☐	☐	☐

	Excellent	Good	Adequate	Poor
Overall opinion of this Kit	☐	☐	☐	☐

Do you intend to continue using BPP Assessment Kits/Interactive Texts/? ☐ Yes   ☐ No

Please note any further comments and suggestions/errors on the reverse of this page.

Please return to: Nick Weller, BPP Publishing Ltd, FREEPOST, London, W12 8BR

REVIEW FORM & FREE PRIZE DRAW (continued)

Please note any further comments and suggestions/errors below

FREE PRIZE DRAW RULES

1   Closing date for 31 January 2001 draw is 31 December 2000. Closing date for 31 July 2001 draw is 30 June 2001.

2   Restricted to entries with UK and Eire addresses only. BPP employees, their families and business associates are excluded.

3   No purchase necessary. Entry forms are available upon request from BPP Publishing. No more than one entry per title, per person. Draw restricted to persons aged 16 and over.

4   Winners will be notified by post and receive their cheques not later than 6 weeks after the relevant draw date.

5   The decision of the promoter in all matters is final and binding. No correspondence will be entered into.